CW00848365

Triathlon for V

Everything You Need to Know to Get Started and Succeed

Copyright 2015 by Triathlon Hacks

Published by Charlotte Campbell

Charlotte is also a contributing writer at www.triathlon-hacks.com

Click here to get your free download on **how I took 17% off my triathlon race performance by training less!**

***

Table of Contents
TRIATHLON FOR WOMEN

Chapter 1:
Why you need to read this book

WHO
RUN
THE
WORLD?

Triathlon is one of the fastest growing sports for women. USA triathlon recorded a female membership of 37% in 2014. It is an amazing event offering new challenges, well-rounded fitness and an amazing feeling of accomplishment when you cross the finish line. Triathlon makes you a better athlete and a better person. You will learn amazing skills- like grit, focus, time management, nutrition and sticking power.

There are distances to suit everyone. If you are just starting out and have not exercised for a while- do not get daunted by the thought of an Ironman. A super sprint consists of 400m swim, 10km bike and 2.5km run. Most people could finish that without much training. But if you fancy a 2 hour race or a 6 hour race or a 16 hour race… they are all available!

Who is the book for?

This book aims to help you if you:

- Have not started triathlon yet and are thinking about taking the plunge

- Have done a few races and are looking to improve your performance, be more structured and scientific

I will cover topics like:

- Swim, bike and run and how to get better at each discipline

- How to achieve super quick transitions

- Important nutritional needs for women

- Female specific strength training

- Training during pregnancy and how soon after to resume

- Gear you need

- Bike maintenance

- How to develop mental toughness

- Managing and avoiding injuries

- Mastering brick sessions

If you are starting out on your triathlon journey and start to tell people you are training for a triathlon, you might encounter shock, wonder, awe and a lot of people telling you that you are crazy and all the reasons why you should not do it!
So before you involve other people, make sure YOU are clear in your goals and WHY you want to do it- or your resolve will melt away very quickly and you will be back at the cafe eating donuts and sipping on extra large lattes agreeing that you were crazy to think you could do it.
Everyone has a different reason for joining triathlon.
These are some of the common ones:

- Lose weight

- Achieve a personal challenge

- Do something for myself

- Improve fitness

- Gain new friends

- Charity event

- Look younger, gain a hot body

- Stay fit to keep up with my kids

Whatever your reason, you can achieve all your goals and you will gain a whole lot of unexpected benefits along the way. The sooner you start, the better.
It does not have to take over your life, it will not stop you seeing your family or getting ahead at work.
You can do it at your own pace and train as little or as often as you want. You can join a club or train with a friend or simply train by yourself whenever you can squeeze it in.
   Some of you may have thoughts about triathlon in the past but had thoughts which may sound a little like these...

- There is too much to learn
- It's too difficult
- There is too much gear to buy
- I can't swim
- I can't change a tire

- I will be the only girl
- I don't look good in lycra
- There is too much to get to grips with

All of these thoughts are perfectly natural but as you will see from this book, nothing is further from the truth! You can start now, with minimal fitness, without great expense and without a ton of technical knowledge.

This book will help you dispel all these fears and get you moving in the right direction. Anything else you need to know, I will tell you in this book.

By the way, I know this because I have been where you are. I have been at the stage of thinking about it for years and never feeling I was quite good enough or fit enough to enter a triathlon.

I was always generally fit, but the thought of entering a triathlon was a massive step.

It was too easy to put it off, and think next year I will do one ("when I am fitter" or "when I have more time"), but inevitably, next year came and went.

You will never be "fit enough" or "feel ready enough" or "have enough time"

The best way to approach it if you have been thinking about it for a while- is to just enter one- give yourself 3-9 months depending on the distance you choose and your fitness level- book it, pay for it and write it on your calendar. Then you have to do it!

Remarkably somehow you will find time, make adjustments and get it done.

Once you have momentum, you will be amazed at how quickly you find yourself on the start line with a pit of nerves in your stomach. Then not so long after you will be saluting the air as you cross the finish line on one of the best days of your life full of pride, grateful to the world for being so amazing and signing up to your next one.

My journey started when a friend just entered me into one and told me I had three months to get ready. Of course I pretended to be annoyed but I guess deep down I was secretly pleased because maybe I never would have "got around to it".

Anyway with the focus of the race approaching, I was suddenly motivated, and spurred on. At the time there were no books at the standard I needed. There were a few highly technical books for advanced athletes doing ironman but that sort of knowledge was way above my head and quite frankly, too intimidating. I was scared enough already that I did not have the "right" bike and the "right" wetsuit.

Inevitably on race day I was nervous and did not feel ready. The usual thoughts kept popping into my head: "Maybe I can just turn around and go home", "If only I had another month to train". I managed to banish these thoughts and I did the race. I enjoyed it.

No, it was more than that. **I loved it!** I loved every minute. It was hard at times and I was glad when the finish line came but I had a ball...and I was really proud of myself.

In fact over the next few years I was hooked! I invested in the proper gear, read loads of books on training, did lots of training and entered several races, some of which I won!

Anyway the point is anyone can do this. This book is designed to help women from raw beginners, but also women who maybe have a done a few races but feel they would like to go to the next level and make their training a little more scientific. That is what is great about this sport. There is always more to learn, always more to improve on, and it is never boring.

You are at the start of a great new adventure and you do not know where it will lead.

Certainly it will lead to better fitness, new friends, greater self-confidence and improved health. This book is designed to talk to you as a friend.

A few of the books I have come across aimed at women are very patronizing and so basic that they do not really add much value at all.

Hopefully you will find this book easy to understand but also packed with detail, practical tips, ideas for drills and covering a whole range of topics which you need to learn in order to improve like the mental side of racing, nutrition, racing rules and regulations, the kit you need, how to prepare for each discipline and much, much more.

You can absolutely complete a triathlon. Age, fitness, job, skin color or size are all irrelevant. There is no barrier to entry and you will find triathlon is a really great world full of supportive people eager to help newcomers.

Of course you will have questions, be nervous and perhaps overwhelmed but this is natural in any new endeavor- sport or otherwise!

Best of all, I can take you through it step by step because I have taken the same journey!

I never thought I was fit enough. I was averagely fit at school and joined in most sports at school level. When I left university and started working I got busy and did less and less sport, probably like most of us.

But once I was back into it and had a new focus on my new sport there was no going back. I simply love it and urge you to start no matter what level you are at.

Do not let the little negative voice inside your head steal your dreams

So jump right in, read this book, which has already helped so many women get started, and improve in triathlon. It will dispel many of your fears, provide some incredible tips and short cuts and get you started straight away.

So why write a book just for women?

Triathlon is one of the most perfect sports for women. It does not require large amounts of strength, aggression or testosterone.

It is flexible. We can fit it in our schedule between work, family and social commitments.

It gives us a fantastic mix of fitness, strength and competition. Many women I talk to do get intimidated by all the gear at the start line, understanding how to repair a bike, cycling with the traffic on roads, the transitions and so on. All this stuff is easily learnt and is part of the fun.

Forget about being intimidated! Just start- wherever you are, follow the advice in this book, and you will steadily make progress.

Also acknowledge that if this is a new challenge for you- it will be scary!

Great! That is natural.

Often we look back at the last few years and realize we have done nothing scary or taken on any new challenges for a while. It is important to do at least one new scary thing every year or you are not growing as a person. If you do not push your comfort zone from time to time, maybe you are not pushing hard enough.

Make sure you set new goals each year- this is one of the most important things we can do as humans- strive to achieve our full potential. Push your comfort zone.

Especially if you are a mom! You can get trapped in the routine of doing so much for everyone else and putting yourself last all the time that you end up achieving nothing for yourself. Resentment or lethargy can set in, neither of which is good for you- or good for your family.

Of course there is no getting away from the fact that there CAN be a lot of aggression and testosterone in triathlon but it does not require it to compete.

To be honest, in most of the clubs and races I have participated in the men are very supportive and encouraging of the women. We are all the same boat (to some extent), struggling to fit in work, family, training so we all support each other.

We all suffer from fears, injuries and self-doubt from time to time –yes- even the guys!

Although they might not admit it, men are going through the same fears.... many of them know nothing about changing a tire or getting out of a wetsuit quickly. In many ways it is worse for them because they are expected to know this stuff and must never look weak!

There is only occasionally the total jerk- who may make a derogatory comment about a woman in the club or your running style... but it is usually because he fears being beaten by a woman!

But truly, these people are very much the exception- and NEVER let one throw-away remark by a total idiot- get in the way of your dreams, your goals, your fitness and your health. The vast majority of clubs and people in them are awesome and will enhance your life and give you so much respect and confidence, you will wish you started this sport earlier! Incidentally whilst the world record is held by a man, the top girls in the sport beat 95% of men anyway!

The world record time in the Hawaii Ironman is currently held by Craig Alexander in 8 hours, 3 minutes. The top female record for the same course is held by Mirinda Carfrae in 8 hours, 52 minutes. If ANY athlete male or female evens finishes an Ironman- they deserve- and get -total respect. If anyone completes it in under 11 hours- they deserve to be worshipped!

Plenty of women beat very good male athletes so don't ever worry that you can't keep up or you are not good enough! It is just a question of training.

Whilst much of triathlon training is based on the same general principles for both men and women, we do have different physical and psychological makeups so there are differences in the way we should train and prepare for racing. Women have some extra issues to consider along the way. What about pregnancy? Childbirth? Can you still exercise? Is it too strenuous? What about prolapse, urinary frequency, hormones?

Is there different equipment you need? Nutritional needs, racing styles or mental focus that is different to that of men?

The answer is yes and I will take you through these differences and show you how you can maximize your natural advantages.

Once you have completed your first triathlon, you will be hooked and all the initial learning and race day nerves will be worth it. This book will provide you with the insight and tips you need to arrive at your first race feeling confident, and well prepared.

Very often what brings women triathletes to the start line is completely different to that of men.

But even within our own female fraternity there are many differences in the way we train, in the drivers for competing and our physiology. Some women are corporate high achievers and have always been super-competitive and fit, some have sacrificed their own lives for a while to have a family, some have never done anything for themselves and are plagued with self doubt, some have been averagely fit and now want a new challenge or some have faced and battled cancer or serious illness and now believe they can achieve anything.

Whatever the reason, you are now in the right place.

Are there women only events?

If one of the things putting you off is entering races with men, you will be pleased to know there are many women-only events. Whether you agree with this or not is fine, whether this is for you or not is fine- just know that they do exist.

In the USA the Danskin women's triathlon series in the USA boasts 200,000 participants since it started in 1990.

Activate Your First Secret Weapon

Many female triathletes think that they should just train based on "how they feel" that day. They think that they will remember last week's sessions and even last month's sessions.

This is highly unlikely.

Memory can be very vague as the police know when they ask a group of people who watched the same event, to recall what happened one hour earlier. There are many different versions of what actually happened.

How much less likely will we be able to recall what happened last week or last month?

So with our very pressurized time limitations of work, family, training, social activities and so on, a training journal will help you maximize each session and only do highly effective training rather than just junk miles.

Junk miles by the way are a waste of time, add nothing to your strength or fitness and simply increase your likelihood of being injured.

As you develop a profile of your training, you will start to identify areas you are weak in, times of day you prefer, the best things for you to eat prior to a run and so on.

It is important to track as much information as possible after every training session.

For example you should write down:

- the type of training you did
- average heart rate
- power output
- distance
- steady state versus interval training
- what time of day
- the weather conditions
- how well you slept
- fatigue
- muscle soreness or any aches and pains
- how you personally felt beforehand
- how you felt afterwards

- what you ate before, during and after training

Keep going to get as much information as you can. This should not be a chore and should only take a few minutes. You can write it in a journal or some people prefer to log it on a computer.

You should also identify at the beginning of the journal what your goals are for the year, and when you want to achieve them. This will be a massive help when you are planning your training, so you are clear how fit and strong you need to be at certain times of the year, so you schedule in time to taper before an event, so you schedule in recovery after hard sessions or races.

Be clear about what you want to achieve then break this down into six month, three month and monthly goals. This will help with your training plan.

You should identify WHY you are doing this. This will help you stay motivated when it is raining outside and you simply want to stay inside under the duvet (this happens more frequently than you might think). You need to remember your "why" and get up and train anyway.

The reasons might include:

- My friends are doing it
- To lose weight
- To complete a new challenge
- To remain fit and healthy

- To beat my 17-year-old son

Whatever the reasons are, write them down on page one of your journal so that when it is raining and you do not want to go cycling or running, simply read your "why", put your shoes on and go.

You know you will feel great afterwards.

An accurate training journal is one of the most powerful training tools you have

It will allow you to look back, see what has worked, what hasn't worked, what your body responds to best and areas you can improve.

Also you get a massive motivational boost from just seeing how much you have improved over the year. It will make all the hard training worth it. You will not believe how much your body can change and adapt.

A training journal will also warn you about possible injury or sickness, because often you will notice warning signs in advance. For example, if a cold or flu is developing you may notice a higher heart rate for less effort a week before you develop symptoms. This is a sign to take it a bit easier. You may notice a tight feeling in your calf when running several days or weeks in a row. You may need to get a sports massage or increase your stretches to prevent an imminent calf tear.

Most importantly, keep it simple. If it becomes a chore, you will give up and not do it at all. It really should only take you a few minutes after a session.

As with most things in triathlon, discipline and consistency is everything

There are some online programs available but if you do your own excel spreadsheet or use a pen and paper, it is free, easy and so very powerful. If you have not started doing this, start today!

Smashing Obstacles

As with any plan, obstacles suddenly appear.

So, let's tackle them now.

Time

This is the biggest hurdle for all of us. You, like many people, may have a busy career, family commitments, friends and a successful sporting life.

Really examine your day. A 24-hour day consists of 3 x 8 hours.

Let's say 8 hours is for sleep, 8 hours is for work. There is still enough time to do a few household chores, spend time with the family and fit in some training.

Look at areas of your day, which are wasted. See if you could arrange things differently. Be really strict with yourself. Is there wasted time in front of the TV or trawling the internet for stuff you do not really need? Could you do all the shopping once a week instead of going to the shops every day?

Schedule yourself first so you can achieve your goal and fit everything else in around that. No more placing yourself last.

It is amazing how much you can fit in if you have to. Most tasks expand to fit the time we give them. Do not let vacuuming the house or ironing the kids shirts get in before your training.

Know How

This book will hold you by the hand to show you what you need to know. I have been there, done that, made every mistake. This book will help you short cut the typical mistakes beginner triathletes make in order to maximize your time and enjoyment.

Most people do not take the time to prepare much at all. By reading this book, you will know more than most people who have done triathlon for two or three years.

Your mind

There will be many obstacles along the way: the biggest one is your own mind!

Fear and self-doubt, the little voice inside your head asking:

"What am I doing here? All these other people look so much better than me!"

"The water looks rough. Maybe I should just go home now!"

"How many hills are there? Oh no, I will never make it!"

Guess what, you are not alone. Every woman faces these questions, nerves and self-doubt on a daily basis. Part of training is preparing your body for the challenges that lie ahead, but also increasing your confidence and preparing your mind for the challenge of training and racing.

Do not quit before you start!

Triathlon provides so much variety, anyone can complete one. You can fit it into your busy schedule around work, kids and family commitments and it is a supportive and inclusive environment. There is very little macho rubbish around women appearing at the start line so do not let this fear stop you for a minute!

There are fantastic, well-respected role models like Helen Jenkins and Chrissie Wellington, who have shown it can be done and give us all huge amounts of focus and inspiration. They have high profile careers in their own right with decent sponsorship and prize money.

So let's get you started. Who knows where you could be a year from now?

Chapter 2:
What is triathlon?

Triathlon is a multi-sport event, which involves swimming, cycling and running and the 4th discipline, transition (which is changing from swimming to cycling (T1) and cycling to running (T2)). The race is in that order and must contain these disciplines to be a triathlon.

A little history

The first triathlon was held in 1975 in Mission Bay San Diego. It consisted of 6 miles of running, 5 miles of cycling and 500 yards of swimming. There was no entry fee and 46 athletes took part. Cross-training was not a term that had been coined at that stage.

Then in 1978 in Hawaii, some people were arguing about which discipline required the greatest endurance. At that time Hawaii hosted The Waikiki Rough Water Swim (2.4 miles), The Oahu Bike Race (112 miles) and The Honolulu Marathon (26.2 miles). Originally events in themselves, they were rolled into one to become the 'Hawaii Ironman Triathlon.'

15 athletes competed and just 12 of them finished. A woman, Lyn Lemaire, placed 6th and became the first "Ironwoman". If you want to see an incredible and inspiring Ironman finish to a race, check out Julie Moss on You tube. In 1982 she was nearing the finish line when severe dehydration and fatigue set in. She collapsed just yards away from the finish line.

Kathleen McCartney passed her for the women's title and Moss crawled the rest of the way to the line. Her performance was broadcast worldwide and created the mantra that just finishing is a victory!

But by 1982 the Hawaii ironman attracted coverage on ABC sports and had 580 athletes competing for glory. Now 1800 lucky triathletes compete to earn a coveted spot at this sport's major event.

There are also 29 official Ironman events around the globe and many, many unofficial ones.

Distances

There are various distances involved in triathlon. They range but the official ones are:

- Sprint distance: 750m swim, 20km bike, 5 km run
- Olympic / standard distance: 1.5km swim, 40km bike, 10km run

- Half Ironman, middle distance: 1.9 km swim, 90 km bike and 21 km run
- Ironman: 3.8 km swim, 180 km bike, 42 km run

You will find other distances locally and for your first event you may try a shorter one than sprint. However if you are going to continue with the sport it is a good idea to try and keep to the standard distances so you can measure your improvements and performances over time.

Where do I start?

Most of you will already have a fair idea of what distance you want to start on, what your existing fitness level is and you will also probably have some vague goals.

Have a quick skim through this book and understand the world of triathlon and what is required. If you have not done a triathlon before, a good starting place is to do a sprint triathlon, which is the smallest distance. This will get you started with not too much training and preparation. You can prepare adequately on 5 or 6 hours training a week.

Some people stay with the sprint distance forever. This may be because of time constraints, or because you feel you are more a sprint athlete or shorter distances suits your body shape.

If you wish to try longer distances then the sky is the limit with Olympic distance, half iron man and ironman distances on offer. If you are a true beginner, just stick to sprint and Olympic distances in the first year or two to build your baseline fitness without injury before piling on the mileage.

There is a recent trend for beginners to jump straight into Ironman distance because it sounds sexy, because they are impatient or because they have seen it on TV.

Most of these people get a very harsh reality check (unless they are already very fit from another sport), and end up not completing the distance and never do triathlon again!

The training required for full Ironman is intense so you do need to rearrange some of your life and your priorities to fit this in. It is best to plan this event over a 2-year build up to allow your body to adapt to the mileage without injury.

The important thing is not to worry about this but simply get started on the fun distances now!

Do not wait until you have all the gear, all the strategies and all the training plans set up.

Simply grab your bike and go, grab your swimming goggles and go, grab your running shoes and go. All the details can be refined later.

Success is the result of many small efforts repeated day in, day out

Many people start with their first session or two then stop. I urge you to keep going.

Set a goal, and then write down a plan to get you to that goal and DO NOT stop until you reach it. Part of triathlon training is training your character to do the work even when you do not feel like it.

Accept the challenge, stick to your program rigidly, whether it is raining outside or you just don't feel like it, the feeling of success and achievement when you cross the finish line will taste even sweeter.

One advantage about triathlon training is there is always something you can do. So for example if your legs are tired from a hard run yesterday plus it is raining outside, you can make today your swim session or hit the gym and do a core strength session. It is great to have so many options!

When you train, remember you are also training your mind and your strength of character

Practice sticking to your plans and achieving mini goals. When the voice of self-doubt appears on your shoulder, be strong enough to recognize it for what it is: A total lie!

Fill your head instead with opposite thoughts of how great you feel, how well prepared you are, how much progress you have already made and how great you will feel crossing the finish line.

Time is always a challenge- but once you decide, you will find time. Prioritizing will make you more efficient and gain more energy.

Giving this time to yourself will allow you to give so much more to others. This is a lesson we, as women, need to learn and be reminded of often.

So very often we give so much to everyone else leaving ourselves frazzled, stressed and having achieved absolutely nothing for ourselves. This serves no purpose whatsoever.

Give to yourself first then you will be so much more energized, proud of yourself and able to give more to your family.

Also remember you are not alone.

The world of triathlon is so supportive. There is so much encouragement from clubs, websites, books and forums- you will be astounded.

Any time you feel alone or start to feel overwhelmed, get online and interact in a forum discussion, call a triathlon friend or pop down to a local race and watch all the awesome women who have made it happen and are crossing the finish line with beaming grins on their faces and a major sense of achievement in their hearts.

Resolve to join them and get involved. This book will set out step by step all you need to know and how you will achieve it. It really is logical and anyone at any fitness level can achieve great things. The only question is – do you want to be one of them?

If you have been motivated enough to read this book, you can certainly complete and enjoy triathlon. I am excited for you.... Are you ready?

Triathlon: Is it for super fitness freaks?

In some ways triathlon has done itself no favors in creating an image of crazy people doing punishing schedules, training 6 hours every day, weighing their food, carbohydrate loading and banning alcohol, cakes and late nights. It seems a little excessive!

And yes these myths have come largely from the world of the Ironman distance, which does take up a lot of time, and requires super discipline and commitment.

If you are starting out, a sprint distance triathlon is one of the most balanced sports around. You train nearly every muscle in your body through the three disciplines and gain a good balance of strength and cardiovascular fitness.

Best of all you are never bored! The shorter distances are over in 1-2 hours. This is hardly enough to take over your life but certainly enough to give you a huge sense of accomplishment, great fitness and ideal body weight.

Mindset is everything: If you think about training as a chore that just has to get done and out of the way- then it is unlikely you will last. If you think of it as fun and a break from the kids, the chores and the deadlines, you will love it, look forward to it and get the best out of your training sessions.

Ageing

Any woman can complete a triathlon and grow to love the sport.

This includes you no matter what your age, ethnicity or weight.

As I said before, just start wherever you are and get going. Remember some women do not start until their 50's or 60's and then enjoy a 20-30 year triathlon career of fun, good health and achievement.

So age is no excuse! People from all walks of life compete, so do not let your own preconceptions hold you back. Many triathletes find their times improving year on year as they get fitter and learn more about the sport.

They also gain race experience and improve their mental toughness and stamina. You are never too old or too young to start, so stop thinking about it and start doing.

Why not do something right now? That's right, stop reading, get up and do 10 press-ups then keep reading. Trust me you will feel better.

The most important thing about a goal is doing an action towards it straight away!

What about my family? It will take me away from them

If your partner is into sport or fitness, it is great to do shared training sessions sometimes. If you have a family, you can get the kids involved. They could ride their bikes as you jog along next to them or when you take them to swim training, instead of sitting on the sidelines wasting an hour of your life, jump in the adult pool and do a swim set yourself.

If you do have kids they will be proud of having a fit mum who looks amazing amongst the other parents, young, fit and fresh faced, instead of one who can only talk about the soap operas on TV, the special offer on the chocolate biscuits and how tired they are all the time.

Start Training

Base training is the first focus of any training plan, then endurance, then speed and finally power. As you proceed through your training you will make change to intensity, volume or speed to train different energy systems and different muscle types and shift from largely aerobic training to anaerobic.

I will teach you how to structure the best workouts to get the most out of them. You will be training harder and smarter. The one thing you need to ditch is junk miles. These are miles just for the sake of it, which achieve absolutely nothing except potential injury.

Before you commence each session you will know what the outcome is and how it will get you closer to your triathlon goal.

As a general rule you will need to do 15-20% swimming, 40-50% cycling and 25-30%. Of course if you have a particular weakness, do spend time practicing that one and if necessary get coaching in it.

Chapter 3:
The Secrets To Simple Bike Maintenance

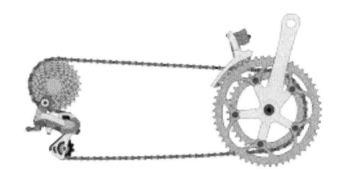

What are you like at bike mechanics?

Changing a tire?

Fixing a bike chain?

I have put this chapter towards the front of this book- as it is really important. Both for your own safety and for self-respect you need to be able to do simple things to your own machine. In the past, many of us have been guilty of letting men fix our bikes- as this is a dirty job and sometimes fiddly and difficult. Often women are encouraged not to learn how to maintain their bikes. This is ridiculous, old fashioned and stupid! You do not have to become an expert in everything but you do need to be able to change a flat tire and do a quick weekly check. In a race situation if you get a puncture, you will need to quickly and efficiently change your tire so please learn this and practice it many times in training. You are not allowed to get outside help.

It is important for your own safety as well. Imagine you are out in the middle of nowhere with a flat tire, unable to get back. Do you really want to rely on help from a passing stranger?

Please make sure you are self-reliant.

Practice this many times. Maybe the first time you fix a puncture- it might take you 30 minutes. As you get better you should get that time down quickly so you can change it quickly if this happens in a race. It also may happen on an isolated road, miles from anywhere, freezing cold with driving rain.

You should be able to fix the tire within 1-2 minutes so your fingers don't freeze and be on your way.

The pros can change a tire in 15 seconds.

Some bike shops run bike maintenance tutorials, which are really worthwhile. You will be spending a considerable amount of money on your bike. It is your responsibility to maintain it and ensure it is in good working order.

Never go for a training ride without a couple of spare inner tubes, repair kit, tire levers and a light bike pump. Chances are, if you do carry this stuff as a rule, you will never need them but we all know what happens the day you leave the house without them.

By the way, these days it is always a good idea to carry a cell phone for safety. Some longer rides can take you quite a way out of your area, so tell your family or a friend where you are going, how long you will be gone and when you are expected back. If possible try to find some friends of a similar standard to cycle with. It is more fun and much safer.

Essential Bike Tools to carry:

- Pump
- Patch kit
- Cell phone
- Spare inner tubes
- Tire levers
- ID: medical information like blood group, allergies, emergency contact information
- Some money
- Wear a helmet, ALWAYS!
- Spare tubes

Check you buy the right size! Spare tubes come in various sizes so make so you check your tire and buy the correct size. The size will be written on the side of the tire.

If you get a flat, simply replace the tube, look to repair the flat when you are back home. Warning: always carry two spare tubes and a patch repair kit. It is not unknown to get two flats on the same ride. It is also not unknown to immediately get a flat on the new tube because it pinches the rim! Very disheartening!

When you take the old tube out carefully check the wheel for debris, nails or glass. Try to identify what caused the puncture and make sure it is still not inside the wheel otherwise, as soon as you pump up the new tube, it will puncture immediately and you will be extremely angry with yourself.

When you are back at home, repair the puncture. Find the hole by inflating the tire then feeling the air coming out against your face or hearing the hissing sound.

Clean your chain and your bike when it needs it. This really depends on the conditions. Wet, damp conditions will collect dirt and grit off the roads more easily. Salt will get into your bike if you are in a coastal area, so wipe it down regularly. Take a few minutes at least once a week to look it over and do some basic maintenance. It will add years to the life of your bike.

Check the bottom bracket and chain. Check the rear cassette (the cogs on the back wheel), the front forks, front and back brake pads and the derailleur. Wear old clothes that you don't mind getting covered in grease – because they will. Have some old rags handy and an old toothbrush. Buy a chain cleaner from the bike shop and a degreaser. It is best to take the wheels off once a month and give them a proper clean. But do the basic wipe down each week.

In a race situation, if you get a puncture, you will need to quickly and efficiently change your tire so please learn this and practice it many times in training. You may not get help from spectators or you will get disqualified. You should aim to do this in less than 1 minute and be on your way.

Before Every Ride:

- Pump up your tires (there will be a recommended pressure in psi on the side of the tire). Know what this is and re-inflate your tires to this each time. Usually for racing bikes it is around 100-120psi. This will help you go faster and will prevent punctures

- Make sure you clean and lube your chain

Apply degreaser. Wipe off with a clean rag and go over the links with an old toothbrush. Pay attention to the cogs and cassette too. Dry it off then re-lubricate with a chain lubricant. While here check the chain for signs of wear or rust

- Clean Your Bike

  Wet, damp conditions will collect dirt and grit off the roads more easily. Salt will get into your bike if you are in a coastal area, so wipe it down regularly. This will add years to the life of your bike.

- Check for rattles and loose nuts and bolts

- Regularly check the tread on the tires and for signs of wear and tear

- Check the seat post is on firmly and handle bar stem is tight

- Check the wheel spokes: if they are bent or damaged, get the bike shop to replace them

- Gears and chain: check that all the gears work and the chain is free from dirt, dryness and rust

- Brake cables: check for over stretching and fraying.

Also check the brakes. If the lever is fully engaged before the brake pad stops the bike, you may need to replace the brake pads.

- Brake pads: check for cracking. Brake pads should contact the rim directly and squarely

Bike Lingo

Bicycles come with their own language and terminology.

Here are a few common terms you should know:

Bottom bracket: the bearing assembly the crank set spins on

Crank set: the big mechanism ring that the pedals are attached to

Front and rear derailleur: the system and the front and back cogs that moves the gears

Headset: where the handlebars attach to the frame

Cassette: the cluster of sprockets that attaches to the hub on the rear wheel

Serial number: can be found underneath the bottom bracket. Make a note of it as it identifies your bike for insurance purposes or theft.

What To Check Once A Month

Wheels: Make sure the wheels are properly fastened and aligned correctly.

Steering: Check for looseness and tighten where necessary

Pedals: check they spin freely and tighten if necessary

Gears: check they all work and move up and down smoothly (It is best to leave any gear repairs or adjustments to a mechanic)

Frame: inspect the frame for any signs of damage

Wear old clothes that you don't mind getting covered in grease. Have some old rags handy and an old toothbrush. Buy a chain cleaner from the bike shop and a degreaser. It is best to take the wheels off once a month and give them a proper clean.

How to Change a Tire

If you can confidently change a tire in less than 2 minutes, feel free to skip this section.

If you do not know or have not practiced for a while, time yourself, then come back to this section if you need to. It is not difficult but it can be a bit fiddly-so it is a good idea to practice once a month.

This is a very important skill to have as a cyclist and will make you self-sufficient on the road and race ready in an event.

1) Remove the wheel from the bike. Most bikes now have quick release. So that is easy but where people go wrong is they forget about the brake calipers. So gently use the lever to release the brake calipers, unscrew the bolt on the axis and remove the wheel.

2) Unscrew the valve and deflate the tire.

3) Place a lever under the edge of the tire and hook the other under around a spoke. Do the same thing a few inches away with another lever. You may need to do this one more time then you should be able to put your fingers underneath the tire and remove the tube.

4) Pump up the flat tire quickly and examine it for glass or debris. Remove the offending object carefully. If you can't see anything, check on the tire itself and run your fingers (carefully) around the inside of the wheel checking for

debris. You will be extremely frustrated if you pump up a new inner tube only to have it puncture straight away as there was still glass left in there.

5) If it is clean inside, slightly pump up the inner tube so it has some structure. This will make it easier to insert. Start with the valve then insert the tube carefully.

6) Alternative: you may choose to repair the tire or you may have got more than one flat and need to repair the tire. Mark the hole with chalk. Use sandpaper from the puncture repair kit to scuff around the area where the hole is to help secure the patch to the tube. Spread glue evenly over the hole and wait for glue to dry until it feels tacky to touch. Place a patch over and apply pressure. Or use glueless patches!

   Hopefully, you will not have to do this very often but it is good to know how to do it.

7) Now it is time to get the tire back on. Make sure one side of the tire is back in place. Also some tires have an arrow that tells you which side the tire should go to ensure the tread is facing the right way. Check your tires well in advance to see if your tires are like this. You don't want to go through all this only to realize later then have to start from scratch. The arrow points in the direction the tire rolls when the wheel is back on.

So now you should have the tube in, and one side of the tire in. The tricky part is the other side of the tire.

Once you get to the last few inches, keep trying with your fingers. Be patient, breathe and keep working it on. If you need to use tire levers, you may pinch the new tube and get another puncture so take extreme care.

CO2 cartridge

These are brilliant for speed of changing a tire. It inflates the tube almost instantly to the right pressure. The problem with hand pumps is they are exhausting to inflate and difficult to get the right pressure.

In a race you want to make it as easy as possible to not waste valuable energy, and to be honest even on a training ride, you will be grateful for them. Once you use them once, you will never go back.

Of course – do not carry them for a race if you have never used it before. Practice before hand so you are familiar with it.

There are two main parts: the nozzle and the inflator.
Get the inflator with flow control- This means you can stop/start the pressure as you wish. Without flow control means you only have one shot to get it right.
I buy the one with flow control- it just makes sense.
The cartridges come in 3 sizes 12g, 16g and 25g. The smaller ones fill tubes up to 90 psi, the larger ones to 120+ psi.
They also come threaded or non-threaded. Threaded have less chance of going wrong. You can buy everything in a kit- to make sure they all match for purpose.
If you buy bits separately make sure you buy threaded cartridges and inflators with threaded and non threaded with non threaded.
So let's go through how to pump it up.
You still need a bit of air in the tube to get it to fit correctly. With the nozzle on the valve, it is time to screw in the cartridge. It should screw in easily at first then come to a slight halt. This means you are about to break the seal and release the CO_2 into the tube.
Once you do this it will inflate in about 1.5 seconds.
Depending on whether you have racing wheels or not, you may need to add one more cartridge – as riding with low pressure increase risk of punctures.
Clean everything up and take your litter with you- If you discard kit or litter in a race you will get a penalty.
Slide the wheel back onto the frame, and tighten it gradually checking the wheel is aligned evenly between the brake pads.
Make sure you ensure the brake pads are back in their correct position and make sure the brake levers are back in place.

Very important last step that no one tells you

When you get home, deflate the CO_2 and re-inflate with regular air. CO_2 dissipates through rubber and you will lose half your psi by the next day.
Also repair the puncture and make sure you have at least two spare tubes ready to go out for your next ride.

How To Repair A Broken Chain

Along with a flat tire, this is probably the next common
occurrence that occurs to cyclists. This sounds difficult but it is
actually fairly simple to do.
You will need a chain tool- they are on most multi tools. If not,
you should get one.
Fixing a bike chain on the street is no harder than fixing a flat
tire if you are prepared.
The most common way your chain breaks is by pedaling full
force at the same moment that you are shifting your front
derailleur.
So try to ease up on the pedal force when changing the front
derailleur to reduce the chance of this happening.
Each link of a chain is held together by a steel pin / peg. With
the chain tool (or a hammer) you can push out and push in the
pins, allowing you to remove or attach links.
Fixing a broken chain amounts to removing the broken link
and re-attaching the remaining ends. On bikes with derailleurs
there's enough extra links that you can remove a couple
without a problem.
On a single-speed bike you probably won't have enough slack
in the chain to remove a link, you'll need to borrow some links
from an old chain or else buy a new one.
Step 1
Flip your bike over so you can get to the chain more easily.
Step 2

Take a look at the two broken ends. One end (possibly both)
is damaged and needs to be removed. What you will do is to
remove 2 segments of the chain at the damaged end.
You need to remove 2 segments instead of 1 because the two
types of segment alternate. If you just remove 1 segment you
can't re-attach it.

Step 3

Place the chain into the groove in the chain tool at the spot you want to disconnect. If you are replacing a worn but non-broken chain you'll do the same thing here.
Turn the screw on the chain tool to start pushing the pin out of the chain. Be careful to keep the pin on the chain tool lined up with the pin on the chain, sometimes they like to slip around a bit.

Don't push the pin all the way out! Only push it just far enough so the chain comes apart. You need to leave the last bit of the pin in the chain so you can push it back in later.

Step 4
Now feed the chain back onto your sprockets. It helps a lot if you have a friend who can hold the two ends in position while you reattach them.

Use the chain tool to push the pin back in.
This is the trickiest part to keep the tool lined up with the pin.
Note: if you are putting on a new chain here, many new chains come with a special link that makes the first-time installation possible without pushing any pins in.
Once the pin is in, the link you just attached will be stiff. Work it back and forth until it loosens enough to bend around the gears.

Summary

So there are the basics.

It will take you just a few minutes to do a weekly maintenance. Definitely practice changing a tire quickly, time yourself if you have not done it much before. Put it on your schedule to do once a month and get your time down.

It is one of the skills triathletes require in races that no one tells you about until it is too late.

Get you know your bike and all the moving bits. The more you can do yourself, the better your bike will perform.

No one will look after it as well as you. Plus you will get a lot of respect from any guys you are out cycling with it you can confidently and quickly fix your own mechanicals.

Chapter 4:
Winning Nutrition for Women

As athletes, we spend an enormous amount of time training, planning our training, preparing for training and recovering from training.

But how many times do you actually focus on nutrition?

Of course, many times I am sure you have had the thought "I'm absolutely starving!" and can eat copious amounts of food whilst staying slim much to the envy of your friends.

But as you progress in your triathlon journey, it becomes more and more important to plan your nutrition in advance.

Anticipate when you will be "starving" so you can have the best quality foods on hand and not be at risk of hitting the candy bar.

Understand your body's training and recovery needs- and be more structured about the amount of protein, carbohydrate, fat and micronutrients that you are consuming.

And what about water? Hydration needs to be thought about and planned for maximum results.

Whilst it may sound like a lot of work, it is not difficult to get the basics right and with a tiny bit of thought, the significant improvement in your performance will surprise you.

It is like putting poor quality cheap petrol in a Ferrari.

The car may look pretty but if it chugs along slowly with black smoke pouring out the exhaust and breaks down, it is not quite as impressive!

Your body is your engine-AND your home!

Make sure you fuel it with the best nutrients and it will reward you with better performances, a leaner, stronger frame, quicker recovery from hard sessions and a much slower ageing process!

Many triathletes make the mistake of just eating a lot of junk food, fast food and take out because they train so much they do not tend to put on weight.

Sure, you can get away with this for a while but you certainly will not be getting the best out of your training sessions. Also you may be storing up problems for later on like early onset of degenerative diseases.

You do not have to make radical changes… instead gradually makes improvements and tweaks here and there until your develop a system that works for you. Sometimes a radical overhaul is too much, so you do nothing.

So just focus on one thing at a time until that becomes a habit, then pick the next thing.

As you start to notice how much more energy you have and how much better you feel, you will gain momentum and it will be much easier to think of food as fuel and reach for the higher quality real food instead of stuff that came from a packet.

Gradually Develop Your Nutritional Plan

I suggest you start adding your food to your training journal early on so you can start to note patterns of food that agrees with you and rubbish food that upsets you or makes you feel sluggish.

Make a note of the food, the quantity, how soon before training you ate, if you ate anything during training, what you consumed after training.

All these details will build a picture over time to give you accurate data to draw from to develop a proper plan that works for you.

Most athletes pay no attention to their food at all and simply grab whatever they can find at the time. When it comes to wanting to improve their performance or plan what they should eat on race day- they have absolutely no idea and choose things at random.

It is not surprising that one of the biggest causes for poor race performances or even DNF's (did not finish) is getting nutrition or hydration wrong

Many athletes:

- Eat or drink too much during the race and get stomach cramps

- Try a new sports drink or gel at the feed station which they have not tested and get stomach problems

- Don't eat or drink enough and run out of fuel

Over time you will start to hone exactly how much fuel you need prior to a race, how far in advance to eat, how much you can consume during a race and what is the best fuel for recovery after a race.

You will KNOW what to eat every week, during training periods and especially during a race instead of guessing!

Nutrition can be a very tricky area for most people. It can become complex fairly quickly.

Remember you do not have to be a nutritional scientist. Keep things simple at first. Listen to your body and how it feels and how it responds- write it down.

If you are just starting out, do not get bogged down in too much detail. Do not count calories excessively and do not be weighing your food.

What you eat and when you eat plays a huge role in how you perform and how quickly you recover. Most of the advice on sports nutrition is aimed at men. Whilst most of this is good advice, women do have different needs so I have aimed to compile this as comprehensively as possible.
Women have a different attitude to food than men. We have been socialized to be concerned about weight, being thin, not eating too much. This can lead to serious eating disorders. Men have been socialized and encouraged to have a big appetite. This is celebrated.

Also as a woman trying to juggle family, training, work and friends, she can tend to eat on the run or simply grab convenience foods as she does not have time to cook.
As a triathlete, you are placing MORE nutritional demands on your body, so you need to be eating more not less.
An average woman requires approximately 2000 calories a day but remember you are not an average woman. Most female triathletes need to aim for around 2400-2800 calories per day- depending on distance and training hours.
You also need to be sure you are getting adequate protein, fat and carbohydrate plus a wide range of vitamins, mineral and micronutrients to support muscle repair, bone strength and many metabolic processes.
   Be sensible, cut out junk food, drink more water and eat natural fresh food.

If You Are Overweight

One of the biggest reasons for starting triathlon for many women is to lose weight. For many others, losing weight, reducing body fat, increasing lean muscle tissue is simply a welcome bonus to doing something they love anyway.
Some female athletes are conscious that losing weight will get them drastically improved performances. So whatever your reason for losing weight, it is important to do it sensibly.
If you are trying to slim down and restrict your fuel too much, you also won't perform at your best as you will simply not have enough fuel to sustain your activity.

If you take it to the extreme and lose too much weight, you may develop low energy, lack of periods (amenorrhea) and poor bone density. Too much calorie restriction does not give the body enough energy for basic functions like metabolism and daily living. The brain senses this and sends a signal to the body to lower production of estrogen and other reproductive hormones.

The lower energy intake also increases cortisol, a catabolic hormone which negatively impacts bone and muscle growth. Estrogen plays an important role in calcium absorption so lower levels decrease the amount of calcium in the body, which prompts the removal of calcium in the bone. This increases the overall risk of stress fractures, osteoporosis and fertility problems.

Constant dieting and restriction of nutrients also slows recovery from injury and normal repair of muscle tissue. Many athletes do not know how to lose weight correctly and simply skip meals or cut out whole food groups like meat or dairy. This can reduce the intake of adequate levels of protein, carbohydrate and healthy fats necessary for normal bodily functions and to fuel athletic endeavors.

If you skip proper meals with real food containing protein, carbohydrate and fat, you will also be missing many micronutrients like zinc, iron, calcium, B vitamins and magnesium required for growth, immune function and repair. So select food from wide variety of food groups.

It is best to target any weight loss in the off-season or in the base training phase when there are less demands on the body.

For most people, an actual "diet" won't be necessary as simply increasing their training will increase the energy requirements sufficient to lose weight.

Just make sure you do not increase the donuts, cream cakes and sugary drinks. Gradually try to eliminate these empty calories and prepare healthy snacks before hand. Fruit, cereal bars, bagels are good examples.

Also make sure you drink plenty of water along the way as it is easy to mistake thirst for hunger.

The purpose of nutrition is to fuel the body

Female athletes also need to pay attention to nutrition to ensure a healthy menstrual cycle and strong bones. The menstrual cycle uses additional energy. We need to make sure we prepare for this so fatigue does not set in and also to ensure regular cycles. If a female athlete lacks adequate nutrition, she may lose her periods altogether. Poor nutrition also results in brittle and weak bones.

As a general rule a female athlete should eat 40 calories per kilo body weight or 20 calories per pound- minimum!

Athletes lose more electrolytes through perspiration such as sodium, potassium and magnesium than sedentary people. Intense activity also requires more anti oxidants to be replaced to protect the cells from oxidative damage.

Energy Drinks

Some people live on caffeine, sugar and energy drinks. Whilst they do give you a boost in the moment, they actually drain energy from you long term. They destroy your adrenal glands, disrupt blood sugar and result in a huge energy crash after the high.

These are not foods that give us high energy. Some athletes use caffeine or energy drinks during a race or during very long cycles rides to enhance performance which is fine in the short term but it is not good to use these excessively to get through every day or to supplement short training sessions.

They also rot your teeth and can lead to weight gain.

Why female athletes need to include fat in their diet

Many female athletes are obsessed with their weight – for the obvious need to look good in lycra! But a healthy weight will also ensure better performance. For weight loss it is better to reduce empty sugars than fat.

Cutting out fat can have a negative impact on performance. Healthy fats are an enormous source of energy delivering nine calories of energy per gram as opposed to carbohydrate and protein delivering four calories per gram.

During training, you will be teaching your body to burn more fat as a fuel source than carbohydrate.

Fat also prevents the breakdown of muscle protein and promotes faster recovery after a workout. In addition fat plays an important role in normal bodily functions. Typically a female athlete should be eating 30-35 % diet in fats. Eat from a wide range of fats including red meat, dairy, nuts and oil.

There is a misconception that eating fat will make you fat. This is not true. Overall fat levels in an average American diet have fallen but obesity and fat levels have skyrocketed.

Researchers from New Zealand found athletes with a higher fat diet (30%) had much higher endurance. Researchers from University of Buffalo found that athletes with a higher fat diet got less injured than those on a low fat diet.

Weight loss is best done slowly. Simply changing your diet to healthy whole foods and increasing your exercise levels will have you losing all the weight you want at a steady and gradual pace.

Reaching for diet supplements can be dangerous. You do not need to do this. Most of them are unregulated for safety and efficacy and some have been linked to harmful side effects like heart attacks and stroke.

Train your body from the inside out. Eat a variety of natural foods and keep your fluids up all the time. Athletes who consume adequate calories and nutrients train better, recover quicker and are less susceptible to illness.

Good Sources Of Fat:

- Avocado

- Oily fish-salmon, mackerel, sardines, trout

- Eggs

- Sunflower, pumpkin seeds, flaxseed oil coconut oil

- Almond or cashew butter

- Cheese

Most Female Athletes Need More Protein In Their Diet

Athletes require more protein than sedentary populations. Most male athletes are obsessed with getting more protein. But sometimes, female athletes need more encouragement. Maybe this is because the obsession with protein comes from the body- building world of packing on excess muscle, which most female triathletes are not seeking to do.

However we do need a good amount of protein in our diet for:

- Maintain muscle mass

- Repair muscle

- Preventing hunger pangs

- Increase number and size of mitochondria (energy powerhouses)

Nothing is better than protein the way nature intended complete with essential amino acids, the correct proportion of fat and minerals already included. Chicken, beef, eggs, nuts and dairy contain more than enough protein for an athlete.

If you are going for muscle strength you certainly require adequate protein but not excessive protein. More is not better.

The recommendation for sedentary people is 0.8g/kg body weight.

Athletes should have 1.2-1.4g/kg. Also contrary to popular belief, endurance athletes need more protein than strength athletes to maintain aerobic metabolism and muscle repair. If they do not have enough protein the body leaches it from the muscle tissue and this gives many endurance athletes that gaunt drawn appearance.

So an example of a typical day could be a couple of eggs at breakfast, a can of tuna at lunch and a large chicken breast at night. Rather than counting grams you can ensure you have some protein with every meal.

It might be harder to achieve if you are vegetarian or vegan. If you do eat eggs and dairy, you will be fine. But if you don't, you may need to supplement with appropriate protein powders. Plant sources include beans, lentils, nuts and seeds and some leafy vegetables like spinach.

The Carbohydrate Dilemma

There are three sources of fuel for the body: carbohydrate, fat and protein. The primary fuel for energy is carbohydrate. Carbohydrate is burned more efficiently than fat or protein. Energy can be released from carbohydrate three times as fast as it can be from fat.

The body stores carbohydrate as glycogen in the muscles and liver. However its storage capacity is limited so it needs to be replenished during exercise.

Female athletes need to eat at least 5-7 g carbohydrate per kilo body weight for moderate exercise (1 hour exercise per day).

For high intensity exercise, of 1-3 hours per day, up your carbohydrate intake to 6-10g per kilo bodyweight.

For extreme intensity, >4-5 hours, up your carbohydrate intake to 8-12 grams per kilo body weight.

However carbohydrate needs vary depending on activity levels so you should vary your intake depending on intensity and duration of training. Overall a diet high in carbohydrate (about 60% of your daily intake) is important.

Carbo-loading fact or fiction?

The science of carb-loading has changed somewhat in recent years. It is not just about ploughing down plates of pasta. But done correctly it can make a huge difference in endurance events like triathlon.

As mentioned before, the body can store enough glycogen for about 90-120 minutes of exercise so if you are doing sprint triathlon, you don't need to change your diet significantly. Just maintain a good, well-balanced, healthy diet and fuel your body properly on race day prior to your event.

However for longer distances this science is important to stop you hitting the "wall" and running out of energy.

Carb-loading used to involve a program starting the week before the race. It involved hard exercise combined with carbohydrate depletion for three days in the final week. The next 3 days would involve very little exercise and overloading the carbs prior to the big race.

The theory behind this was it would encourage the body to store more glycogen

However it did not really work. What happened is the athletes would become very tired due to the carbohydrate depletion and hard exercise, lose morale and focus. Then they found it hard to stuff themselves to the required level at the end, feeling bloated, heavy and sluggish.

So the recent advice is to keep to your normal diet and exercise routine (obviously you are in the taper phase anyway) and simply add more carbohydrate to your diet in the last 3 days.

In general you need 5-7g of carbohydrate for every kg body weight. In this carb-loading phase go for 8-10g for kg of body weight.

To reach your carbohydrate target eat little and often throughout the day rather than going for huge meals.

Remember the important distinction it is not about eating MORE calories overall. It is about increasing the proportion of carbohydrate in your diet

Most athletes eat slightly less overall during the last week because they are tapering and do not have the huge energy expenditure they had in previous weeks.

Examples of high carbohydrate meals include:

- Grilled chicken and rice

- Wholemeal toast and peanut butter

- Large bowl of spaghetti

- Cereal and milk

And yes still include some protein, which will give you an energy boost and slow the digestion of carbohydrate, releasing energy slowly – perfect for endurance events!

Carbs During The Race

In any race over 60 minutes, taking in carbohydrates in the form of bars, gels or drinks is a good idea to spare muscle glycogen. For events longer than 2-3 hours, you will need to take in carb/protein mixes as studies have shown they help athletes perform significantly better than carbohydrate only drinks or food.

Avoid eating refined carbohydrate foods like cakes, biscuits and pastries too often containing trans fats.

Food timings

There are also decisions about when to eat based on when you train. As well as ensuring you get enough carbohydrate throughout the day, the timings of ingestion can dramatically help sports performance and recovery.

Ingestion before activity can help top up carbohydrate levels in glycogen and blood glucose- particularly for early morning training sessions and if the event is over 90 minutes long.

Consuming carbs during exercise can help delay fatigue and the decline in mental and physical performance.

Carbohydrate after exercise is essential to restore glycogen levels as soon as possible to enable optimal performance the next day. Incomplete or slow restoration of glycogen levels will lead to incomplete recovery and reduced performances in subsequent days.

The amount and exact timings will depend on the distances you will cover and your intensity as to how close to exercise you eat and whether you eat during exercise.

Ideally you will want to eat about 2 hours before you train. However in the practical world, if you train before work, it may mean a quick banana in the morning, some water, then go training, then off to work with a sports drink and bagel en route.

It does require preparation.

Definitely have something prepared for straight after training so you do not have a window of no fuel. If you do not have fuel within a 30 minute window post exercise it can take you up to 3 days to recover instead of a couple of hours. This is very important.

For example:

Two or three hours <u>before training</u>:

- Bagel and bowl of pasta
- Yoghurt and cereal bar
- Chicken breast and baked potato

<u>During exercise</u>: To prevent depletion of carbohydrate stores, which results in fatigue and poor performance, consume carbohydrate-rich sports drinks (for events over one hour).

<u>After exercise</u>: Consuming glycogen speeds up muscle repair by replenishing glycogen stores. There is a "carbohydrate window" of about 30-40 minutes, which is immediately after exercise. This is the most important time to replenish stores to get maximum recovery. Studies show this makes a massive difference in rapid recovery. Eat bagels, fruit, or energy bars.

If you start to run low on carbohydrates you will experience "bonking" where your body runs out of useable energy. For this reason we need to take on carbohydrate before and during exercise.

Iron needs for female triathletes

Triathletes depend on efficient delivery of oxygen to working muscles. Iron carries oxygen to our muscles.

Iron deficiency is prevalent in female athletes.

Symptoms include: fatigue, headaches, dizziness and poor immunity.

Iron is responsible for:

1) Transporting oxygen to the brain and the body

2) Creating red blood cells

3) Controls the release of energy from the cells

4) Healthy immune system

Did you know when you sweat you lose iron with each droplet?

If you are looking to boost muscle or endurance, it will be an uphill battle without adequate iron intake.

Iron deficiency starts slowly and is exacerbated by poor nutritional intake. Prolonged deficiency causes the body to tap into its reserves. This will severely impair the ability to carry oxygen around the body.

Iron needs are higher in athletes, especially female athletes:

Women need 15 mg iron compared to men 8.7mg due to iron losses in menstrual blood. Anemia – inadequate iron levels is not uncommon in female athletes.
If you have these symptom consult your doctor. You will be given a blood test and you may be prescribed iron tablets.
Iron deficient anemia is more common amongst vegetarians as less of the iron found in plants is absorbed than from meat
If you are vegetarian be sure to have 6-8 eggs a week as well as 2-3 servings of vegetables a day that contains iron – like spinach, lentils, dried apricots.
These should be eaten with a source of vitamin C to increase absorption like fruit or spinach.
If you are vegan, have a tablespoon of black molasses each day.
The body is unable to manufacture iron so we must eat it daily.

There are two sources of iron- heme or non-heme.

Heme is the iron found in animal products such as beef, lamb, chicken and seafood.

15-18% of this iron is absorbed. By the way red meat has three times the iron than chicken and fish.

Non-heme sources are plant-based sources such as cereals, legumes, green leafy vegetables, nuts and dried fruits. Absorption is around 5%.

Iron rich foods:

- Lean meat 1-3mg
- Beans and lentils 3-4mg
- Fortified breakfast cereal 18mg
- Spinach 2-3mg

Calcium

Calcium helps build strong bones and teeth. Calcium is perhaps the most important mineral for athletes. A recent survey of 10,000 athletes found that 50% do not regularly eat 1000mg of calcium per day. The recommended dose is 1000mg-1500mg per day.

This concern is particularly important in female athletes as inadequate calcium can predispose to hormonal deficits, weak bones and a predisposition to fractures.

Good sources include yoghurt, milk, cheese, spinach and broccoli. (1 glass of milk provides 300mg calcium)

Sodium

Sodium helps cells retain water and prevents dehydration. Sodium also enables ATP generation. For events lasting longer than five hours, especially in hot weather, hyponatremia (dangerously low sodium) is a real concern. Most organized events have aid stations with salty snacks. Anyone out for more than a few hours, especially on a warm day, should make sure to get some salt from snacks and fluid-replacement drinks. In general you should not need sodium tablets as most foods and electrolyte drinks will have enough supplemental sodium

Zinc

Zinc aids in post-exertion tissue repair and in the conversion of food to fuel. Both male and female athletes have lower serum zinc levels compared with sedentary individuals. Studies correlate endurance exercise with periods of compromised immunity—zinc depletion may be one reason.

Those who train without days off lose zinc even more quickly..

Athletes should take 30 to 60 mg zinc daily.

Oysters, liver, seeds and dark chocolate contain zinc.

Vitamin E

Vitamin E is one of the most important antioxidants for athletes. Endurance athletes have an increased need for this vitamin because their cells undergo more oxidative damage. Vitamin E has not been shown to benefit athletic performance but athletes should ensure they take 400-800 IU per day.

Good sources vitamin E include dark, leafy greens, avocados, nuts and seeds and shellfish.

Eat Often

The key to good nutrition for athletes is to snack regularly throughout the day. Always have a snack to hand like nuts, seeds, berries, low fat yoghurt, a bagel or piece of fruit. It will stop you getting too hungry then reaching for rubbish food. As an athlete, hunger strikes at any time.

Prepare in advance and leave the pies, sausage rolls and chocolate bars for the spectators!

Nutrition periodization

If you are a beginner, you may skip this section and focus on getting the above guidelines correct first.

If you have done a few triathlons already, you keep a training journal and stick to a training plan, implementing nutrition periodization can do wonders for your performance. It is a much more structured, professional way to match your food requirements with your training requirements.

There are specific phases in building up to a key race of the year to ensure your peak at the right time. Your nutrition needs will change with the goal of the session.

As your training moves from base training to more intense work, to tapering, your nutrition needs to change. Fuelling your body for triathlon is more difficult than fuelling a car. With a car you fill it with the same stuff each time it is empty.

With triathlon you are fuelling several different energy systems from a choice of 3 different main foods groups and many micronutrients and trying to balance adequate hydration without over doing any one-food group.

During **base training** you are laying down the groundwork of aerobic conditioning. Workouts are typically long and intensity fairly low. A sample ratio could be carbohydrate 60%, protein 13% and fat 27%.

During the **build phase** you are doing longer and harder efforts and spending more time at lactate threshold. You will need more carbohydrate and less fat as a source of energy. Overall don't skimp on calories here.

During **racing and peak training phase**, you are doing high intensity training. Drop the fat content to 15% increase the protein to 17% for muscle recovery and carbs to 68%.

During **recovery phase**, increase the protein and decrease the carbohydrates.

You need to focus on muscle repair. You do not want to be putting on weight.

Summary:

- Don't let a bad diet let you down and waste all the training you have done all year

- Pre plan your meals each week so you are not tempted to grab a take away or hit the sweets because you have nothing left in the house and don't have time to go to the shops

- Eat to win. Eat to recover. Eat for fuel. Keep your energy levels up

- Keep hydrated – often the brain mistakes being thirsty for being hungry.

- To stay lean all year-round, learn to eat when you are hungry but when you are full, STOP eating. There is no need to stuff yourself just because it is there!

- As a busy athlete juggling three sports, it's easy to eat on the go all the time. Sit down to eat meals and switch off distractions to fully enjoy your food and be aware of exactly what (and how much) you are putting in your body.

- Eat (healthy) fats. Fat is satiating and essential for

optimal health, functioning and energy. This means you should eat fatty foods such as salmon, nuts, olive oil and coconut oil.

• Get decent sleep. Calorie consumption increases when you are tired. Getting a full night's sleep will keep you on track.

• Don't skip meals to lose weight. Getting overly hungry will just raise cortisol (stress hormone) levels and make weight loss harder. Plus you are more likely to eventually break down and binge on sugar. Slow and steady is the rule for lasting weight loss.

• Get enough protein. Protein is one of the main differences of men and women's diets. Men are often obsessed with protein. Women are not bothered or think it is only for body builders.

Chapter 5: Strength Training for The Girls!

It is a mistake to dismiss strength training as a man's game. As women, we need strength training EVEN MORE than they do. And the good news is, because most of us are traditionally weaker than the chaps and tend not to do strength training as a rule, when we do strength train, our gains are exponential!

Strength training will make a huge difference to your training and race performance and will also help improve your technique and stamina and prevent injury. It will also improve your resistance to lactic acid build-up.

We all know triathlon is a great endurance sport. We train for hours to refine and enhance our stamina and our ability to keep going at a steady pace for long periods of time. In the beginning most triathletes spend as much time as possible on the bike, swim and run to gain experience and endurance. This is proper and correct.

However as you advance in your training, the quickest way to get faster and better is through gaining strength as well. Even if you can just commit to finding one-two sessions a week in your schedule, it will pay huge dividends in terms of injury prevention, race performance and improved endurance. During the season, do not lift weights to the point where you are so sore you cannot train for 2-days. Save this for the off-season.

Simply do enough to improve and complement your training.

You will be so grateful for some strength on hilly courses when others are failing on the hills and you can easily overtake them, or on a windy day when you cut through the wind resistance like a knife or at a critical point in the race when it counts, you can accelerate and go with the lead bunch, or make a break or sprint to the finish line faster than your friend.

Strength gives you such a significant advantage that I add it to every triathlon-training program I design because it is that important. It is also a massive advantage because most triathletes do no strength training whatsoever. Crazy I know!

If you do strength training, you will be miles ahead and make progress more quickly without getting injured.

Strength training is smart and gives you maximum results for minimum time input.

Common Myths About Strength Training

Many women have been misled about strength training.

This is a shame because it helps to solve some of the issues women agonize about **all the time**!

Strength training is one of the quickest ways to lose fat.

Strength training is amazing for anti-ageing.

Strength training will give you incredible sport performance.

Myth #1 Strength training will make be bulky

This is rubbish and does not happen. Those people who do have incredibly big muscles have to eat an enormous amount of calories each day to get big muscles.

They actually have to set their alarm and wake up at 3am to have another meal because they require more calories than they can physically eat during a normal day.

They also have to ingest or inject extra supplements to stimulate the muscle growth response.

The average triathlete with their sports drink, doing 2 x 30 minute strength sessions a week does not even come close. In addition the actual training you will do is aimed at gaining strength not gaining bulk. Most females do not even have the required levels of testosterone in the body to achieve muscle bulk.

Myth #2 I don't have time

Strength training will save you time. You will get far more out of a 30-minute strength training session than another 2-hour bike workout. You will gain strength to attack the hills, improve your lactate threshold, improve your speed towards the finish line and improve fatigue resistance.

Strength training is the most efficient workout you could do.

Studies done of high performance Ironman athletes show they can complete the Ironman in sub-10 hours by employing triathlon training programs of just 10-12 hours a week instead of usual 20-25 hours a week. They achieve this incredible feat by doing more strength training and short high intensity bursts rather than the long, slow plods of 3-4 hours.

Myth # 3 Older women should not strength train

Complete garbage! In fact strength training keeps you young.

Many studies have shown:

The older you get, the more strength training you should do

As we age, we tend to experience a decline in muscle mass. This is due to a natural decline in growth hormone after the age of 30 years old.

Strength training preserves bone density, metabolic rate and muscle mass. Without weight training, your muscles will atrophy and lose mass with age. If you do no weight training, you can expect to lose at least 15% muscle mass between your 30s and your 80s.

This will only happen gradually- so in your 60s or 70s you will notice it is more difficult to climb a flight or stairs, get out of a chair or lift the shopping out of the car.

Strength training will prevent risk of falls and broken bones, help maintain metabolism, prevent arthritis, and maintain better hormonal regulation.

The older you get, the MORE strength training you should do.

Myth # 4 I don't know what to do

This is more a poor excuse rather than a myth. Not knowing what to do can be fixed in about 20 minutes.

Obviously I will give you here the best triathlon specific strength training exercises that I do and I encourage my clients to do.

There are many others and many variations as well.

If you are new to strength training, it might help to hire a personal trainer once or twice to show you initially how the machines work or how to set up your barbells or dumbbells.

Myth # 5 I Can't Afford to Get Injured

Strength training prevents injury. By strengthening up your tendons, bones, joints, muscles you are strengthening all the support structures of the body. Strong people get injured less.

Strength training also allows you to address the muscle imbalances that develop by hours of cycling, pounding the pavements and swimming laps. All good athletes at a decent level do strength training to prevent runner's knee, Achilles problem, swimmers shoulder and back pain.

Cyclists and runners spend many hours a week doing squats, lunges and leg presses. Swimmers do lots of shoulder and back strength work. And they all do core-strengthening as an essential.

It does not have to take long, 30-40 minutes is all you need to experience noticeable improvements.

Likewise any patient who comes to a clinic with one of these conditions will get given a strength-training program.

Starting out

If you have never done strength training before, start very light. You need to get your body used to the movements and you do not want to get injured. Be consistent.

If you go to the gym, great! Many triathletes do a gym session on the same day as their swim session if the pool is at the gym. This saves time.

If you do not like the gym, you can still do most of it at home with light-weights, body weight or resistance bands.

Obviously you are not trying to bulk up so you are looking do to sets of 8-12 reps. The weight must still be relatively heavy, approximately 75% of your maximum weight.

You are not looking to add yet another aerobic workout here

In the beginning there will be a little trial and error to see what weight you need to lift.

Start light and go up slowly if it is too light. Aim to fit in 2-3 short sessions per week. You do not want to be so sore from weights that you can't do your other training the next day.

It is about training smarter, not harder!

I will go through exactly what you should do. So even if you are a gym-hater, there is no need to throw strength training out the window. Just adapt some of the exercises to do it at home!

The Best Triathlon Specific Exercises

We are all pushed for time so I will only discuss the best exercises here, the ones that will make the most impact for triathlon. We are looking to do relevant multi joint exercises. Of course there are others you will come across at different times that can be incorporated once you have the basic moves.

Basic Squat

These should be done with your feet hip-width apart, your feet straight, a bar bell on your shoulders or dumb bells in each hand (In the beginning just body weight is fine too). Bend at the hips, keep your back straight, look straight ahead and bend your knees to approximately 80-90 degrees. Push back up to the straight position. You should have no pain in your knees or your back.

Make sure your knees do not collapse inwards. As you improve, increase the weight you lift.

Do 12 reps. Repeat 3 times.

These are important for powerful cycling and running. Squats are also a great exercise for your core strength. Keep your core engaged during the movement to protect your back and squeeze your gluteal muscles as you push up.

Leg Press

If you do go to the gym, a great alternative is the leg press to squats.

Get someone to help you set yourself up correctly. Start light. Make sure your knees go straight over your feet, not collapsing inward.

Push your knees straight, then let them come back to approximately 90 degrees.

Do 12 reps. 3 sets.

As you improve, increase the weight. Start light and see how you feel the next day before going too hard, too soon.

When you get good at this, you can halve the weight and do single leg presses.

Good exercises include things that simulate your sport. Leg exercises should be predominantly one-legged. If you think about it, both running and cycling are sports done with one leg in front of the other. Why would you train them together and not out in front of you?

Lunges

Lunges are a fantastic exercise, specific to running and cycling- one leg is in front of the other.

Step forward with one leg then bend both knees to 90 degrees.

Repeat 12 times. Perform 3 sets.

Initially use just body weight. When this feels comfortable, add dumbbells or a bar bell.

Deadlifts

Deadlifts are one of the best exercises for getting a firm butt, leg and a strong core.

They are an awesome fat burner too as you are recruiting so many large muscle groups. You don't need to lift too heavy. All good runners do deadlifts.

Use the bar only or light dumbbells.

Technique is very important-Keep your back straight, stick your bum out when you bend over and then straighten your knees and squeeze your gluteal muscles.

Keep your core engaged the whole time to protect your back.

You should not have any back pain. If you start to lift heavier- get a trainer to check your technique.

Do 12 reps, perform 3 sets.

Back strengthening

This is important for maintaining a good cycling position, especially up hills when pulling on the handlebars. It is good for maintaining upright posture when running and good for swimming as well.

Seated row

Grab the bar or resistance band. Pull towards your chest, keeping elbows close to your body. Do not sway; keep your back still by using your core muscles. Return to start position. This exercise can also be performed with exercise bands.

12 reps. Do 3 sets

Chin ups

Chin-ups are an amazing exercise for shoulders and backs. It is great for swimming but also strengthens up your back for long hours on the bike. It helps overall posture as well.

Everyone should be able to lift their own body weight. However for some reason a lot of women find this one hard. If you go to a gym, they usually have an assisted chin up machine.

You can take off 20-40 kgs and do assisted chin ups. As you get stronger, take more and more weight off until you are doing chin ups without help

Repeat 15 times, Do 3 sets.

Chest Strength Exercises

These are brilliant for the pull-through stroke for swimming.

Lie on your back, stabilizing it with your core muscles. Lift the bar (or dumb bells) up straight, and then lower back to chest. 12 reps, 3 sets.

You can lift kettle bells instead of a traditional bar – perfect for triathletes.

Press-ups

The press-up is one of the best exercises ever invented! Even if you never go near a gym, do add this exercise to your routine. Great for shoulder stability, core stability, back stability.

It costs nothing and you can do it anywhere. There is NO excuse for not doing this! This upper body strength is important in the swim, the bike and the run.

Go for stamina- 3 sets of 30 reps.

If you cannot manage to do them on your toes, start on your knees, then progress as you get stronger.

Calf strengthening

If you are prone to Achilles tendon problems or calf strains, add this in. Calf raises on the step or calf raises with dumbbells.

3 x 30 reps, stand on step, drop your heel below the horizontal then push up all the way to your tiptoes. Repeat.

Plank

And of course every time you do strength training, you will do your lovely core workouts, which are important in ALL the disciplines and will make real differences to your race times. The plank is one of the best.

Again this requires NO equipment, costs nothing and there is no excuse for not doing it. It is great for maintaining your swim form, preventing back pain on the bike and ensuring you maintain good posture for your run.

Lie on the floor on your tummy. Prop yourself up on your elbows and toes. Check your back is straight.

Hold 3 x 2 minutes.

Of course there are plenty more strength exercises you can do, and I am sure if you go to the gym already, you will know some of these. Rotate the exercises so you use different muscle groups. And change the order each time so your body does not get used to it.

Remember strength training reverses the ageing process!

This is so important that I will repeat it: **strength training is essential if you are a woman,** more important if you are over 35 years old and even more important if you are trying to improve your performance without adding more hours to your training.

Even if you do nothing else in this book but apply the exercises in this chapter- your triathlon performance will sky rocket. It is that important!

Chapter 6: Successful Swimming for Triathlon

It is time to get into the nuts and bolts of each discipline and learn how we can optimize, improve and excel at each one. If you are a beginner, there are many things to get your head round. Swimming, for most people is one of them. Triathlon involves a lot of skill as well as fitness.

Many triathletes cannot swim a stroke at the beginning. So do NOT let this stop you.

For many women swimming is their strength. Women tend to be more patient with learning technique than men who want to muscle through everything. If you develop good swimming technique, you will easily be able to power past many men who are stronger than you.

The feeling will be amazing!

Swimming is an amazing antidote for the body to all the cycling and running. It gives your legs a break, strengthens your core and back muscles and develops great arm tone. As long as you don't permanently smell of chlorine, you will look forward to your swim sessions.

If you actually cannot swim a stroke, I suggest booking some lessons and scheduling some regular time to practice.

You can get an idea of how to swim from books, DVDs and internet resources but swimming is so technical that it is likely you will pick up bad habits that you are unaware of. Use these resources as back up for your face-to-face lessons.

One to one feedback is the fastest way to improve at swimming

Swimming well is ALL about technique and time spent learning this at the beginning will save you so much anguish later. In triathlon conserving energy at the beginning is critical as you will still have to complete two more sports after the swim.

Unfortunately many triathletes finish the swim completely exhausted and struggle to finish the bike and run. Aim to make the swim effortless. When you are training, aim for efficiency.

Once you have had some lessons, regular practice is essential.

When you observe a poor swimmer in a pool- there is a LOT of flapping and splash and awkward body movements side to side and up and down.
There is very little or no glide at all.
It looks more akin to a washing machine turned on full power- a lot of spinning but going nowhere fast!
However when you observe a great swimmer like an Olympian- there is very little splash, there is a lot of gliding, they use long, slow deliberate strokes. It looks effortless.
Once you have the basics and can swim a few lengths comfortably, look to join a master's swim squad or a tri club.

This will help you concentrate on triathlon specific drills and swim sets. Joining a squad will also help you train properly and with varied intensity instead of aimlessly going up and down the pool at a relaxed pace.

Even if you are a good swimmer- a couple of "style correction" coaching sessions per year are really valuable to keep improving.

Olympic swimmers still have coaches and video many training sessions and races to observe their form and see where they can improve. Never be too arrogant to take advice.

Open water starts

Most triathlons are held around lakes or the sea, few are in pools so open water swimming is the discipline triathletes need to develop and get used to.

Open water swimming terrifies many hard-core triathletes and is one of the biggest obstacles for beginners thinking about their first triathlon.

Open water is a world away from the comfort zone of a nice warm swimming pool doing a few laps following a black line up and down.

You must cope with the demands of currents, waves, temperature and seaweed, not to mention other competitors.

Also there is the prospect of a "pack start" where hundreds or thousands of triathletes start a race together. It can be very daunting if swimming is not your strongest discipline and you can get a lot of splashing and kicking around you.

Having said that, it is a skill you can learn and practice – and who knows- one day maybe even get to like!

Tips for Easy Open Water Swimming

Sighting

One of the major skills you must learn is called "sighting". This is where you lift your head out of the water every four or five strokes just before you breathe and see where you are heading. Look out for the buoys as markers.

However if the water is choppy seeing the buoys will be impossible. So make sure before you start the race, you pick out some fixed landmarks on the land to guide you. If you go off course for a few hundred meters it can quickly drain your energy AND your morale!

For example you may see a building you will aim for on the way out as you head west along the bay, then a boat out at sea then, when you turn around, you might aim for the clock tower back on the shore.

The worst thing you can do is follow another swimmer thinking that they know where they are going, because if you are having trouble then they could well be having the same problems and have less of an idea how to solve them than you do. Make your own plan and stick to it.

After you have improved your basic swimming technique, sighting is something you will need to practice in training. Add it to your drills once a week.

Sighting Drill

Swim 500m- with 25m normal swimming, and 25m "sighting". Every 4-5 strokes lift your head; try to keep moving forward as you do this without disrupting your flow. Make sure you don't actually stop to look up- this will be exhausting.

So focus on staying as horizontal as you can, keep kicking, lift up, take a quick look and then get your head straight down again and get back to your normal breathing rhythm.

Very different muscles are required to sight- so if you do not practice this- you will find in any open water swim- you will become fatigued very quickly.

This is a great tactic for getting ahead of your competition as most people will not practice this. You will find towards the end of the swim, many will fade away, while you will still feel strong.

Position in the pack

When there is a bunch of swimmers, it is not uncommon to get kicked which can really spoil your race especially if you get kicked in the face. If you are a strong swimmer, swim hard at the beginning and get away from the pack. If you are not a strong swimmer then let the better swimmers go ahead so you can focus on your race with less bother from them trying to swim over you.

Some people have the strategy of starting on the edge of the pack so they are not bunched up in the middle and this can also work.

Know the course in advance

Doing some homework about the course and the conditions is always a good idea. Try to do a few swims in similar conditions. If it is a lake swim, find some local lakes and swim the same race distance.

Always be safe and swim with buddies and make sure there is someone on land watching you with a cell phone and / or safety devices.

Likewise, if it is an ocean swim, practice some ocean swims. Get used to the currents and temperatures and learn to relax in the ocean.

Do not make race day your first ocean swim!

There is enough going on and enough pre-race nerves without adding the stress of a new environment to the mix.

If you have the opportunity to check out the exact stretch of ocean or lake before the race, this is a great idea. Chat to the locals or the lifeguards about the current and tides. Plan your strategy.

Check if the current is strong and which way it is going. If, for instance, it is running to the right then make sure that you start the race on the left end of the start line, then swim with your sight on the left side of the buoy. You will be pulled to the right by the current and have to fight it much less than if you started at other end of the start line.

Another strategy is to start at the side which you breathe on, so for example if you breathe to the right then maybe start with the pack on your right so you can see them.

Of course if you have learned bilateral breathing, this will not be a problem.

Races are generally pretty safe these days, and there are precautions to stop any serious injuries in the sea. However incidents still sometimes occur- so take open water swimming seriously and ensure you get as strong as possible.

Take Advantage of the Draft

Drafting during the swim portion of a triathlon is completely legal. There are actually two ways you can draft off another swimmer. One is swimming directly behind a lead swimmer and the other is swimming in the wake of a lead swimmer.

And both can be very effective in an open water swim. If you were to swim directly behind a swimmer and close to her feet the result would be a "pulling" effect. Or you can choose to swim to the side of another swimmer and benefit from their wake.

The advantage is massive- you will save 2-4 minutes off your time and arrive at T1 with a lot more energy in the tank.

Of course to get the advantage of the draft, you need to be in the pack or close to other swimmers, so you will also have increased risk of getting "accidently" kicked in the head, so be careful.

If you are a new swimmer or nervous of open water, I advise staying away from the danger of getting hit and just swimming your own race.

The 9 Secrets to Amazing Swim Technique

Start swimming training early in the season. Swimming requires practice, practice and more practice. Do not leave it thinking you can "catch up" later. Start early and be consistent. No matter how hard you train, if you have poor technique, swimming will always be a struggle.

Just because you are fit for running and cycling does not mean you are fit for swimming. Many athletes who a super fit in another sport are shocked at how breathless they get just swimming 25 meters.

Also on race day anxiety, nerves and cold water can sometimes make breathing very difficult. You will be a whole lot more in control and ready for the bike if you are confident and strong in your swimming.

1) Frequency

Frequency is important. Frequent shorter sessions will help you become a better swimmer faster than a long session once or twice a week.

This will help you develop a "feel" of the water. This will give you that sense of power and control in the water; the sense that every stroke counts and gives you significant forward propulsion.

2) Relaxation

The key to good powerful swimming is relaxation. Allow yourself to play in the water a bit.

Push off the wall and see how far you can go under water. Let yourself sink down to the bottom without any panic then slowly come back up.

Hold onto the edge and practice breathing out while your face is in the water (blowing bubbles) and turning your head and inhaling air.

Power and speed in swimming come through relaxation and being streamlined.

How often do you see swimmers training where a huge, muscular, fit-looking man is being out-lapped easily by a skinny, 14-year-old girl?

Answer: all the time!

You do not need to pack on upper body muscle to swim fast. Focus on technique and the speed will come.

Drill:

Try swimming a few laps with very relaxed arms. Over exaggerate the relaxation. Make sure your arms are not stiff or clenched. Practice soft entry into to water with minimal splash. During the pull through, remain relaxed. Focus on feeling the water as you pull through.

3) Reduce Drag

A major rule in swimming is reducing drag. Your head can cause a lot of drag. Aim to be as streamlined as possible. Don't look forward. Instead, always imagine you are swimming downhill and look down at the bottom of the pool. Imagine leading with the top of your head, not your forehead.

Tennis Ball Drill:

Practice swimming with your head in the proper downward position by finding a tennis ball-sized inflatable ball and placing it between your chin and neck. Practice swimming and breathing while still holding this ball between your chin and neck.

Imagine your core is a rigid pole while you are swimming. This is one reason why swimmers do not need big arm muscles. It is technique, position in the water and a strong core, which helps propel them forward and does not dissipate energy.

Kicking technique is important too. It will give you forward momentum and also help you maintain your body position-especially in open water racing. Do not ignore kicking sets. Buy yourself a kick board and get busy doing kick drills.

4) Good body position

Good body position is essential to good swimming. A lot of swimmers find swimming exhausting as their legs drop and drag along. This is like swimming with a lead weight attached to your ankles.

The hips should be high in the water and the feet up, kicking near the surface. The problem occurs where swimmers lift their head to breath and swim with their head high.

When the head is high, the legs will sink

The best way to achieve this position is to stretch out in the water and put your head down.

Most new swimmers swim with their head too high. The head should be down with the water level running right across the top, at the crown of the head. Keep the head down while holding it in line with your spine and shoulders. This way your entire front half will also go down in a nice line and your hips will come up. Look down at the bottom of the pool, not forward.

If your head is raised, your feet and legs will drop, and it will feel like a dead weight is being dragged behind you. Keep your head down and your legs will pop up.

Relax. If your body is too rigid while doing any of this, it will cause excess fatigue and will prevent you from developing a smooth, long stroke.

5) Develop Powerful Arms

This does not mean hit the weights room! This means good technique ☺

Think about swimming tall. You need to think about your body slipping through the water with least resistance. When your arm enters the water, think about it entering through a tiny hole with no splash.

Like a springboard diver- minimum splash

Aim for long, relaxed strokes. Many swimmers have short inefficient strokes. When you reach out in front, try to extend your arm an extra inch and rotate your body a bit to get help get more length.

Enter the water in front of your shoulder, not across the midline.

Bring your arm back under you with a bent elbow. This is a much stronger position than with a straight arm. Think about pulling through with all the forearm and hands, not just the hands. Make it as large a surface area as possible.

Also think about pulling your body forward over your hand rather than pulling your hand back towards you.

Closed Fist Drill:

This is a tough one but really gives you a sense of "feel" of the forearm contributing to the forward momentum. It will feel extremely difficult and pointless at first (like most drills!) but persist with it as it really helps.

Try swimming with a closed fist so you can't use your hands! Think about really using your forearm to propel you forward. Swim 50 meters with your fists closed, then 50 meters with open hands, still focusing on getting propulsion from the forearm. The difference in forward propulsion is amazing.

Recovery Stroke

On the recovery part of the stroke, think about bringing your hand through with a high elbow. Do not do a roundhouse action. This is inefficient and wastes time. Again focus on relaxed hands and arms.

Zipper Drill:

A great drill for this is to run your fingers up your side as you bring your arm through like you are doing up a zipper.

As you rotate to breathe, rotate on your axis, do not flail about all over the place.

6) Breathing

Breathing is one of the most asked-about subjects when it comes to swimming.

It is the area most people even very good athletes struggle with.

The biggest mistake beginners make is not exhaling fully when their face is in the water

The key is to blow ALL the air out, and then breathe in when your head turns. It should be rhythmic and controlled.

Where some people go wrong is they only blow half the air out (or hold their breath) then have to lift their head, quickly blow out then breathe in and then put their head down again.

This makes their legs start to sink because their head is up and they spend the rest of the swim fighting the water instead of gliding through it.

Also this uses excessive energy and so they are forced to breathe harder to gasp for air and the whole problem becomes worse!

Breathing Drill:

Remember breathe in all the way, breathe out all the way.

This is so important that you need to practice this on its own without thinking about your arms and legs and staying buoyant at the same time. So grab a kickboard and swim holding it out in front with both hands- take stroke and breathe as normal- breathe in relaxed, then put your face in the after and exhale fully, then turn your head to the side and take a relaxed breath in. Do your swim strokes as normal.

The other way you can practice is to hold onto the side of the pool and do the same thing- do a stroke, turn your head and breathe in, do another stroke, and breathe out. Repeat focusing on the rhythm of breathing in and out, easily and relaxed.

Do not gasp for breath- there is enough time if you stay calm and relaxed. Practice this, it will pay huge dividends.

The worst thing you can do is take huge gulps of air, then hold your breath for too long. You will be really fatigued.

7) Gliding

Gliding is the KEY to swimming well. This is the major secret which professionals take years to master. Start thinking about it now. The aim is to use the minimum number of strokes to get to the other end. Use the streamlined glide for your momentum. Remember strong stroke, then glide.

Gliding Drill:

When training in a pool count the number of strokes it takes you to get to the other end.

Over the next few weeks try to reduce this number. Michael Phelps (gold medalist Olympic swimmer) takes 7 strokes to get to the end of a 25 m pool. Most swimmers who are reasonably well trained take 13-15 strokes, most beginners take about 20-25 strokes.

When you count your strokes- make sure you do a glide in between each stroke. Slow your strokes down. Start with your arms out in front of you. Do one stroke, bring your fingertips back together, then glide. The do the same with the other arm. Repeat.

It is quite a difficult exercise. If it is too difficult at the beginning- start by holding on to a kickboard to give you some buoyancy.

8) Kicking

Kicking is important. Try to think about the feet as fins helping to propel you forward. Keep the feet and ankles relaxed but your legs strong and taut. Do not kick from the knees.

This is inefficient and fatigues your quadriceps- not a good idea when you have a cycle and run coming up. You only get 10-15% forward propulsion from the kick, but do not ignore it- you need to make sure the legs do not sink. You need to make the kick is efficient and does not drain your energy.

Instead kick from the hips with a strong, stable core.

Make sure your ankles can point so they are not causing negative propulsion. If you have stiff ankles, it is likely you are fighting against yourself. Do some ankle stretches like sitting on your ankles to increase the flexibility if they are tight. Also using fins (flippers) will help stretch your ankles out.

Think about small powerful kicks, not big flailing, scissor kicks that disrupt the streamline of your body.

9) Get Video

If you have swum for a few years, even if you are quite advanced, video is an amazing way to improve. It provides incredible feedback that is meaningful to you.

I know myself when I am in a big swim squad and the coach is pointing out a drill or technique, sometimes I don't know if it applies to me or not.

When you look at a video- you will clearly see whether you are lifting your head or crossing the midline with your hand entry.

One club I joined, hired an under water camera once a month to video everyone. It was amazing to see. The camera does not lie!

But even if you cannot get access to this, get a friend to take a simple video on your smart phone of you swimming. It is so valuable. Watch it later and compare to YouTube video of Olympic swimmers. Or even better if you can show a swim coach who might point out things you are unaware of.

Pool Swim Race Etiquette

Some races conduct the swim in a local pool. This comes with its own challenges.

With several people to a lane on race day, how do you possibly overtake without running into swimmers coming the other way and inducing "lane rage"?

The main area of opportunity to overtake is at the wall when you touch to turn round. If you are competent, you can come in fast, do a tumble turn and push off hard. You will be well on your way before the swimmer in front even knew you were there. If tumble turning is not your thing, you will need to come in fast, touch and push off hard with a quick few strokes to get away and not hold them up.

Whatever happens, do not swim over anyone. Going around people mid lane only works if there are only two of you to a lane. If there are three or more, wait for the wall.

Pool etiquette is to touch the swimmer in front of you on the foot to let them know you are there, they should let you go at the next turning.

The same goes for you, if you feel someone touching your feet, wait at the wall and let them go ahead.

When you are at the race, the marshal in the race briefing will tell you how many laps you must swim. However it is wise to have worked this out beforehand and have practiced the exact length several times. Just use the briefing for confirmation, not new information!

So count your laps as you go. It is your responsibility. Often the marshal will have a system for confirming the number of lengths you have swum and will either shout at you when you have two laps to go or tap you on the head.

Make sure you know what they will do so you do not get a shock ☺

The Gear

Wetsuit

Buy your own gear if possible! Test it, train in it and get to know it.

Taking the time to find a good fitting wetsuit is worth it. A good wetsuit will make you swim faster and make you look hot.

A poor fitting wetsuit will make you look slow and dumpy.

It is possible to hire a wetsuit if it is your first race and you don't know if you will carry on. But once you know you will do triathlon for a season or two- it is much better to buy your own wetsuit.

One of the most challenging parts of triathlon can be getting the wetsuit off when it is wet!

I know of cases where the athlete had to get cut out of their wetsuit in transition!

Some athletes apply Vaseline around the neck, ankles and wrists to ease this. This can save you valuable minutes.

Either way practice this several times until you can confidently get out of it in less than 20 seconds. The pros do it in 3-4 seconds.

Many beginners take over 10 minutes!

I remember in my first triathlon I was exhausted coming out of the water. I was dizzy and disorientated. I could not remember where my bike was. There was a lot of shouting-marshals shouting instructions, supporters shouting encouragement. It was all a blur.

Finally I found my bike and started to remove the wetsuit. I can't remember the actual time but it felt like forever and was a real struggle! In the end I had to sit on the ground as I was dizzy to remove the wetsuit from my ankles as they just would not budge.

Needless to say, by the time I got on the bike, I was just about ready to lie down in a dark room!

The correct way

Unzip the top of the wetsuit as you leave the water and are running to the bike. Once at the bike take the wetsuit off right down to the ankles in one go (1 second).

Then stand on one wetsuit leg and kick one ankle out (1 second).

Repeat on the other side(1 second).

Help you go faster

As well as keeping you warm, wetsuits are also great because they aid buoyancy and so make you swim faster. However in a sprint distance, you need to weigh up whether the time it takes you to get the thing off is worth the time it saves you!

Check with the race organizers about the compulsory use of wetsuits as there are regulations around this. If the temperature of the water is below a certain level they will make you wear one or you will not be allowed to race.

Goggles

Goggles come in various shapes and sizes, get a range if possible and test them out.

It is a good idea to have two pairs- one tinted for sunny days and one without tint for cloudy days. It is also a good idea to bring two pairs of goggles on race day in case a strap snaps or you lose a pair. Make sure they are both anti fog so you can see the buoys in an open water race easily.

Make sure they don't fog up easily, that they are comfortable and that they don't leak. Whilst it is easy in a pool to stand up and remove water from your goggles, it is impossible in open water when you can't stand up.

If you are wearing a race-timing chip, make sure it is tightly secured on a band underneath your suit and on your ankle.

Hand Paddles

These are a great tool for helping you get significantly more power and a much better "feel" of the water. They must be used correctly or you will be inured in 2 weeks.

Do not even consider using hem if your technique is not good or you will exacerbate every biomechanical fault and be off training for 3-4 weeks with shoulder tendonitis.

If used well on the right swimmer paddles will help them develop improved hand entry, high elbows, better pull through and more power.

The paddle should be approximately 10% bigger than your hand.

Kick board

Kick boards are a useful tool in swimming. They can be used as a floatation device. They can help the swimmer focus on upper body technique. It can help aid a good understanding of body position. It can give the upper body a break whilst developing good kicking muscles.

Many triathletes use kick board to help leg endurance and avoid an over reliance on the arms.

Pull Buoy

A pull buoy is a floatation device that you hold between your legs at the top of the thighs to isolate your legs so you can concentrate on arm technique and power.

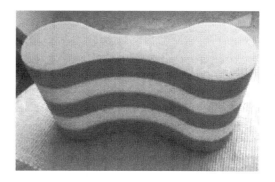

As you swim without help from the legs, make sure you place the hand entry correctly each time, pull through, focus on good body position and engage you core.

A good exercise for technique and drills.

Race Day

Remember your form and your drills!

Incredibly, in the stress of the race and the panic of the start gun, many athletes who know how to swim properly go straight back to flailing about using short, inefficient strokes, lifting their head and gasping for air.

The swimmers who lose their technique will fatigue in 1-2 minutes and come out of the water completely exhausted. Those who come out of the water first are those who remember their technique and get there with minimum strokes, minimum fuss, and a streamlined body.

Remember: relax your breathing, relax your stroke, glide, focus on your technique and do not panic.

Chapter 7:
Girls on Two Wheels

I have already discussed bike maintenance which most people gloss over or ignore, now let's get into which bike, some training methods and technique. First of all if you are a beginner, do not obsess about the actual bike. Many people spend too long agonizing over which bike to get instead of training on one.

If you are a beginner, you do not need the greatest, most expensive bike. Most of the result in cycling comes from the skill, fitness and strength of the rider.

I have competed in plenty of races in the beginning of my triathlon journey where I had a very cheap, heavy commuter bike and was overtaking many other competitors who had very expensive bikes but were still too unfit or simply did not know how to use their elegant machine.

Of course if you have the money, splashing out on a smart carbon fiber bike IS more comfortable and will get you to T2 more quickly…. But if you are at the beginning and do not have a bike (or you have a commuter bike) just get going and get started on any bike.

If you can beg, borrow or steal a friends or neighbor's bike, do that.

My point is do not wait until you have all the gear and have saved up $3000-you can start today if you have a bike (even if you do not have a bike, you can start doing spin class or jump on an exercise bike and find a bike to borrow later on).

At many events, all manner of bikes appear – from the old shopping bike to the second hand monster to the latest carbon bike fresh off the factory floor.

Obviously, the more you spend on a bike, the better your ride will be and the better you will perform. But you do not need a very expensive bike to do a triathlon so do not let that be a reason to put it off for another year.

When the time is right, obviously a bit of investment here will make your training and racing that much more enjoyable. By the way, there are many fantastic second hand carbon bikes on offer all the time from other athletes who may be upgrading so always be on the lookout for these. Also put the word out at the tri club or the bike shop that you are in the market for a second hand bike and you will be surprised at how receptive people are.

You may be able to pick up an awesome bike at half price.

As a rough guide for £500-£700 ($750-$1000) you can get a good quality racing bike with carbon forks. For £1,500 ($2,500) you are very much in the realms of a decent carbon-fiber bike with great gearing.

Aluminum vs Carbon

What is with the carbon obsession?

Aluminum is lightweight, easy to work with, strong and non-corrosive. It is cheaper and easy to produce.

Carbon-fiber is comprised of two material- weaves of carbon fiber and the resin that holds them together. Carbon has similar properties to aluminum but is stronger, lighter and more comfortable. It is more difficult to manufacture and more expensive.

When you look at bikes in the same price range, carbon bikes will be lighter.

Carbon tends to absorb bumps and vibrations on the road better making for a more comfortable ride.

However if you buy a lower priced carbon bike, you may be getting poor quality gearing and group set which offsets the better material fame.

However at the end of the day- you have to ask the question- what is important to you and does it really matter?

It will depend on your budget and what level of competition you are racing at. If you are a beginner just hoping to finish… then spending an extra $2000 to take 15 seconds off your bike time probably is not worth it.

If you are trying to qualify for the Olympic team then 15 seconds quicker is totally worth it…

I will tell you what I did but there is no "right" bike. It depends on your skill level, your budget and your triathlon goals. I did my first triathlon on my commuter bike, which cost less than $100! (I came third in my age group and overtook loads of people on very expensive bikes!)

Once I decided I wanted to do more races, I bought a decent aluminum racing bike for around $900.

I did well on this bike. I had it for about 3 years. I loved it and worked hard on my cycling strength and fitness.

Eventually some friends talked me into upgrading to a carbon bike for around $2000.

I have to say it was much lighter, much faster and more comfortable. I have had this bike for around 8 years.

For the bikes that are more expensive than this, you are paying for things like better bearings, higher quality components, brand name and perhaps a few aero features. The gains are much smaller.

TT

Those who have been in triathlon for a while will have seen (or even own) a time trial(TT) or triathlon bike. These are the ones with a very aggressive riding position and a much more aero bike and position.

Studies have shown there is approximately 22-24% energy saving comparing a road bike set up versus a full time trial bike with aero helmet set up. That equates to 5 minutes time saving over 40 km and 25 minute saving over 180km.

As a compromise, many recreational triathletes simply clip aero bars onto their road bike to gain a bit of aerodynamic advantage whilst retaining the relative comfort and functionality of their road bike.

Do you need to buy a female specific bike?

Women are generally smaller in stature and height than men. We tend to have longer legs in proportion to our bodies, smaller hands and feet, wider pelvic bones, narrower shoulders and shorter arms.

Women-specific bicycles try to adapt to these differences. Generally women's bikes have a shorter distance from the saddle to the handlebar. The gearing is different: most use a triple crank set which is more forgiving on big hills. In some models the handle bars are raised a bit higher to take some load off the lower back. And then there is the design and color which is always more girly!

All that said, try out different models. Chat to the bike shop about a bike fit service, which takes your measurements and fits a bike to you.

I cycle with some girls who are happier on men's bicycles as they are taller and prefer the bike. Individual choice is a must. Shop around. Test out different models and buy something you are happy and comfortable on.

Bike Seat

Some girls buy a "men's" bike and simply buy a more comfortable seat. An uncomfortable ride is pure misery and leads to injury!

Some seats are designed more for female anatomy- but you will still need to test them out as is it not one size fits all. The seat that is suitable for your friend might be very uncomfortable for you.

A soft padded, gel filed saddle might look tempting but once you have sunk into it for a while you may find it creates other areas of burning pain or chafing in the upper thigh.

A harder saddle might actually be more comfortable in the long run, depending on the shape and width of your pelvis.

Generally women's saddles are slightly wider and some have cut out sections to relieve pressure on delicate areas. If the seat is too wide sometimes that may lead to chaffing. Many of the companies give you a money back guarantee so you can test it out and make sure it suits you, so be sure to take advantage of this.

Sometimes chafing still occurs due to sweating or water in the area from the swim. Some women find chamois cream, vaseline or diaper cream applied liberally before a ride helps keep you dry and delicate skin protected.

Bike Fit – Simple Tips

On a 60-minute ride you will probably spin your legs about 10,000 times. It is important you fit the bike correctly or you will soon feel knee strain.

Frame size

Stand over the bike's top tube with both feet on the ground in your cycling shoes. There should be clearance of about 1 inch between the tube and your delicate bits.

Saddle height

Your saddle height should be set so your legs almost fully extend at the bottom of each pedal stroke but not fully extended and locked.

Saddle tilt

Saddle tilt is all about comfort. Try different positions and see what feels best. Slight upward tilt will relieve pressure on your sit bones. Slight downward tilt will reduce pressure on the front of your anatomy.

Handlebar Position

If they are too low, they will make you bend over further increasing strain on your back and neck. Again you need to play around with this a little bit. It depends whether you have a history of back or neck pain as well. The lower and flatter you are, the better for reducing drag. However comfort is the most important thing as you will be spending many hours on your bike.

Cleat position

Misaligned cleats (shoes) may result in knee pain or back pain. Use trial and error to slightly loosen them and adjust them for the first few rides and see what feels right. Try to make sure your toes point forward, not in or out. Make sure your kneecap points directly forward too and tracks over your toes.

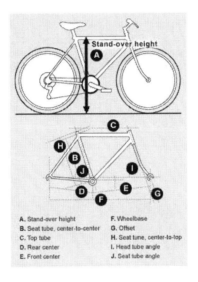

A. Stand-over height
B. Seat tube, center-to-center
C. Top tube
D. Rear center
E. Front center
F. Wheelbase
G. Offset
H. Seat tune, center-to-top
I. Head tube angle
J. Seat tube angle

So play with these suggestions and make several adjustments and tweaks to your bike. If you are really not sure or you experience continual pain on the bike, do make the effort to get a professional bike fit. This will make all the difference.

We Love Our Shoes

Bike shoes contain cleats, which attach the shoe to the pedal. This will give you a faster ride is more energy efficient. Proper cleats in the pedals are very important and make a big difference in Olympic distances and above. If you are a beginner, it is fine to just have toe clips and cycle in your running shoes. This will reduce time in T2 spent changing shoes and be safer if you have not practiced unclipping.

If you do decide to go for cleats, practice is essential as it can be tricky in the beginning clipping in and out of the bike. You just turn your heel out at the back on the side you wish to get off. Give yourself plenty of time in case it is a bit stiff at first. After a few goes it should become second nature and you won't have to think about it.

There are two types of cleats- SPDs and Look system. SPDs are easier to walk in and are on all mountain bikes and some road bikes. Look system are on most road bikes. They are harder to walk in as they have the bolt on the sole.

Both are fine to use and work well. Just be sure when you are purchasing them that your pedals, cleat and shoes all work together with the same system. The bike store should be able to help you with this and adjust the cleats. If you have any knee pain after riding a few hundred miles- a slight adjustment in the cleats can usually solve this problem immediately.

Make sure you practice running with your bike for a short distance with your shoes on and then hopping on, clicking in and riding away.

When buying shoes, make sure you have wiggle room in your toes.

Some cycling shoes are made specifically for triathlon. They offer easy velcro closure, they have a special interior to be comfortable to be ridden without socks and often close inwards offering easy on/off while cycling. Regular cycling shoes are fine too as long as the system is not too complicated for quick transitions.

Prices vary with the more expensive shoes having a carbon element and therefore more light-weight. This is not strictly necessary for most triathletes; focus more on comfort.

Some cycling shoes are marketed at women and are generally slimmer in the heel region for women's narrower heel. But comfort is king- so try them out.

Padded shorts

Soreness, chaffing, irritation and numbness. These are words closely associated with a lot of time on the bike.
Padded cycling shorts are essential for comfort on the saddle with considerable padding to protect your delicate bits. But for race day, switch to tri shorts with less padding that you can wear for the swim, bike and run. This allows for faster transition as you will already be wearing everything you need and can just pull your wetsuit off and be ready to grab your bike and go.
Tri shorts usually have less padding than cycling shorts so it won't feel like you are wearing a wet nappy when you get on the bike!
Tri shorts are designed to be water repellant and seamless. Some of them also offer compressions fabric to reduce muscle fatigue.

Helmet

Remember also a good quality helmet (many race organizers check this and ensure it meets certain safety standards). You are not allowed to race in a triathlon if you do not wear a helmet and it must be fastened BEFORE you get on your bike.

You will be disqualified if you take your bike off the rack and you do not have your helmet on. The best race practice is to put it on top of your bike so it is the first thing you do. When you come to return your bike to T2, leave your helmet on until you have racked your bike.

Most new helmets these days will meet the safety standards, have good ventilation, and be light weight. If you are doing Ironman distances, aero helmets have been shown to significantly reduce drag.

Reducing drag is the name of the game

80-90% of resistance of forward momentum on the bike is aerodynamic drag and 70-75% of that is the rider!

Aero helmets- look silly- are they worth it?

An aero helmet will save to 60-90 seconds over a 40 km time trial. That is significant and obviously multiplied for longer distances. If you are dong Ironman distance and an aero helmet can get to the finish line a few minutes quicker- you will not care how silly you look!

Wheels

Aero wheels make a massive difference. They reduce the watts you have to produce by 50W. Think how hard it is to achieve an extra 50w by training! But they come at a steep price tag. Again for beginners- do not even think about it- just something to keep in mind down the track.

Bike Computer

An important thing to have is a bike computer – Cat eye or Garmin depending on your budget.

You should record accurate data about your mileage, average speed and time to add to your training diary. It also provides you some real time motivation. For example if there is a 40 km ride you do every week and your usual average speed is 16km/hr, you will feel extremely proud of yourself if you do a hard ride and notice your average speed is now 17km/hr for the same ride, then in another month 18km/hr. Of course, allowances need to be made for wind resistance and so on but a good average gives you a guide of where you are.

Also real time data can be important. So maybe there is a hill you normally climb in 42 seconds. Over the season, you may try to get that down to 35 seconds, then 29 seconds.

The Garmin-type computers now contain maps and GPS functions so you can plan your route in advance and don't have to stop every so often to consult maps. (This used to get very awkward when it rained!).

There are also programs you can add to allow you to compare an exact route you did against the time of your friends or other people in your club or locally.

As well as keeping an accurate record of your training and race performances, bike computers are an awesome motivational tool.

Cycling gloves

Gloves are a highly recommended item for training. They make it more comfortable for your hands and wrists with a bit of padding and they are essential to protect your hands should you ever come off the bike. For racing though, most people do not bother as it takes up valuable time getting them on and off.

Superior Bike Technique

Believe it or not there is quite a bit to cycling technique. Cycling will take up the majority of your training time. It also takes up the majority of the time in a race so saving time here is very valuable.

Getting fast on the bike has two main components:-

- Becoming as aerodynamic as possible

- Improving your strength and skill as a cyclist

The stronger you become at it, the more you will love it. The better your technique, the faster you will go with no extra training.

Most people do not consider bike technique at all. They just buy a bike and start pedaling.

Here are the key points to focus on in your next training ride:

1) **Keep your upper body still (check your shadow to watch this)**

Many cyclists move their back, and their pelvis as they pedal. This eventually leads to back pain, knee pain and hip pain and not efficient. Instead try to keep the upper body still and your core engaged.

Push from the legs and gluteal muscles (buttock) without engaging the back muscles.

This will help you use all your energy on going forward not wasting energy going side to side.

2) Relax your upper body

This requires some self-awareness. Many new cyclists are stiff in the arms and tense in the neck. Before long you will have aching neck and shoulders if this persists. As you become more comfortable on the bike, make a conscious effort to relax your hands and arms. Be aware of your neck area and relax it as well.

Neck, shoulder and wrist pain are very common among cyclists. Needlessly tense arms can become a bad habit.

Of course there is place in cycling for using your upper body- sprint finishes or difficult hill climbs for example but for the majority of the ride, continue to remind yourself to relax your upper body.

3) Rhythmic pedaling technique

If you cycle behind a beginner then cycle behind a more advanced cyclist you will notice a big difference even though both are just pumping up and down on the pedals.

There is a smoothness and rhythm in a good cyclist's pedal technique that helps them apply smooth even pressure to the pedals. Think about pedaling in a circular action with even power applied throughout the stroke. Many beginners just use an up and down motion and do not use their hamstrings at all. Instead think of pushing down on one leg as you pull up at the same time with the other leg. Practice steady power and regular cadence throughout your ride.

Also look ahead for hills and prepare gear changing in advance. This will also allow you to maintain an even cadence rather than almost stopping and losing power before you realize and have to scramble for the gears.

A usual "good" cadence for cyclists is thought to be around 90-100rpm. However we must always keep in mind that cyclists are not triathletes and when they finish cycling they are finished.

Triathletes however, have to run after they finish cycling- so do not copy everything from the world of cycling without adapting it slightly for our sport.

In triathlon, a slightly lower cadence is acceptable- around 75-85rpm. This will lead to lower lactate levels and allow better running off the bike. As you become more comfortable on the bike, you will get a feel for what is "normal' to you. As you progress, practice changing gears in anticipation of hills to maintain a similar cadence for most of the race.

You should also be able to reach down for your water bottle and drink while pedaling. Make sure you practice this in every training session. Continue to look forward, keep pedaling and drink when it is safe to do so as you will need this skill for the race.

If you have decided on aero bars, practice getting down on them and back up safely and with confidence.

There is quite a bit to focus on so make a list then practice focusing on one aspect at a time.

Summary

    4) Scan your body as you ride

    5) Upper body is relaxed

    6) Expand your chest and breath deeply

    7) Core engaged

8) Power generated from legs and gluteal muscles

9) Circular pedaling action

Descending Fast

Non-cyclists would think that descending is the easiest thing in the world and something that gives cyclists a "rest".

Actually descending is when you need to sharpen your concentration and it can be extremely physical. A lot of cyclists hate descending as it can be quite scary and as a result a lot of cyclists lose speed, brake too often and get dropped by the group on the descents.

If you are a good descender, you will have a massive advantage.

It involves confidence on the bike, good cornering skills, using your body weight effectively, managing your speed and picking your line well in advance.

Obviously the more you practice descending and cornering the better you will get, so seek many opportunities to practice.

Here are some things to think about to improve your technique and skill:

- Get down on the drops- this will lower your center of gravity, improve your handling and keep you more stable

- Look out for bumps in the road, man-hole covers or loose gravel

- Keep the skills you have learned above going – breathe, engage your core and relax your arms

- Sit slightly off the saddle if you can, this will give you natural suspension

- Depending on the gradient you may need to feather the brakes- so you control the speed. The worst thing you can do is suddenly brake- this could risk throwing you off or if you have someone close behind you, they may not be able to brake in time

- When you go round a corner- you should have you outside leg on the down pedal and the inside leg uppermost. This will enhance stability

- Where you look is critical! The bike will go where you look! So look past the corner where you want to go. Never look at an obstacle- or a tree or a rock or you are likely to head straight for it. Instead look at the space between them or beyond them

- Practice leaning the bike as you corner rather than "turning the handlebars"

- Similar to driving a car or riding a motorbike, try to avoid braking while cornering – this can cause you to skid or overbalance. Try to break BEFORE you get to the corner, then manage your speed through the corner

- Anticipate the line you should take through the corner well in advance. When you are watching cycling like Tour the France or a triathlon, observe how they corner and watch the line they take.

Remember though, you may not often have the luxury of cycling without traffic- so always consider safety first. You may need to brake more in case there is a car on the other side of the corner.

Drop The Pack: Ascending Magic

Climbing is also an important skill. It is not just about strength and fitness though this certainly helps!

Never avoid hills. I know plenty of cyclists who always opt for the flat ride where possible – because "hills are hard!"

This is crazy- yes hills are hard- and they will get you stronger, fitter, faster than your competitors in just a few weeks.

Make sure you do some hill repeats every week.

I have seen good cyclists who can drop the group on the flat, almost come to a complete standstill as soon as an incline begins. It is incredible to watch. Climbing is a specific skill, which needs to be practiced.

Practice standing in the saddle

This is a great thing to do as it gives some of your muscles a rest as it uses other ones.

It also gives your back a break for constantly bending forward.

You will need to play around with your gearing as you will need a different gear if you are standing in the saddle versus spinning uphill in a seated position. Keep your core engaged and as the gradient increases, you will use more and more upper body effort to counterbalance the legs.

Get prepared mentally for ascending. If you approach it with dread, it will feel more difficult. Treat it with respect but know that you can do it. It is best to think about pacing so rather than sprint up it and get exhausted (where you might never really recover for the rest of the race), just take it steady and keep breathing and use your gears.

Standing in the pedals takes more energy than sitting. So use it sparingly- on the last portion of the hill when your gears have run to is a good place to gain a bit more strength to get you to the top. Keep your chest open and keep breathing.

Practice hill reps often, your will be amazed how strong you get quite quickly.

Bike safety

Most of this section will be obvious but do NOT skip over it. It is very important to stay safe whilst you are training. There are a lot of idiots out there on the roads who are in a rush to get where they are going and they really do not care about you, your bike or your life!

They may be texting on their phone or just had a fight with their husband or wife. The sun may be in their eyes or there could be a hundred other reasons why they may not be paying attention. So it is best to assume everyone else is an idiot and take precautions.

Always wear a well-fitting helmet that meets the standards (you will need this for races anyway and the marshals are very strict about checking this).

Obey traffic signs and traffic lights.

If there is a bike lane, use it.

Wear bright reflective clothing including bike gloves, which are a savior if you come off.

At night make sure you have bright lights front and back and carry spare batteries.

In the wet, wear waterproofs but most importantly slow down especially on wet roads and when turning corners. Thin racing wheels are notorious for slipping out from underneath you.

Also be very careful when it has been wet even if it is bright and sunny when you set out. Wet roads and wet leaves on roads can be a disaster waiting to happen.

It is better to be 1-2 minutes later than lying across the road with gravel rash cutting up your leg, a massive bruise on your hip and even worse a collarbone fracture. Take it easy on wet roads!

Also always make sure someone knows you are out for a ride and let them know when you will be back. Carry a cell phone with enough charge left in case of emergency and some cash.

Group riding

Group riding is one of the most enjoyable parts of triathlon training. You are out with your buddies, enjoying the fresh air, enjoying a bit of fun and encouraging each other on. Group riding etiquette is very important for courtesy but also for safety.

Some cycling groups will not let you join unless you know the rules of the road and the common cycling signals so here is a brief overview:

If the group is coming to a stop, signal with your hand behind your back that you are stopping.

Also when riding along, if you spot a pothole or other obstruction on the road, point it out to those behind you. Use hand signals to signal to traffic which way you are turning. When cyclists are riding behind each other, all one can see is the cyclist in front.

So by the time they have suddenly slammed on the brakes it is too late and accidents happen. Signal early and make sure you help your fellow cyclists and they will feel inclined to help you.

If out training with a small group, you may cycle two abreast.

If you are riding on busy roads, ride single file.

Always be courteous to drivers and they will usually be courteous to you.

If you are riding down a quiet road and see an oncoming car shout to your fellow cyclists: "Car front!" so they are aware and will not try to overtake or speed up when it could be dangerous.

Shout: "Car back!" if you are at the back of the group and become aware of a car approaching you from behind to maintain the safety of the group.

Interval Training On The Bike

Interval training is the fastest way to improve on the bike. Consistent stressing of the body's lactate system is the key to achieving a faster race pace on the bike and a smoother transition from the bicycle to the run. You know when lactic build up is at threshold because your muscles ache, your breathing is rapid and your whole body is yelling at you to stop!

Lactic acid is produced in normal exercise as a waste product of muscle. When it is being produced faster than the body's ability to carry it away, you will experience the lactic burn that athletes fear.

Training at lactate threshold gets the legs used to this sort of pain and improves the body's ability to clear it quickly enabling you to cycle at higher intensities for longer. Instead of going for long steady state rides all the time, intersperse them with shorter, harder rides.

For example cycle easy for 10 minutes. Find a good long road clear of traffic where possible and pedal as hard as you can for 2 minutes, then recover with gentle pedaling for 2 minutes. Repeat 5 times.

As your lactate tolerance increases reduce the rest period and increase the workload. For example: pedal as hard as you can flat out for 3 minutes, recover 1 minute. Repeat 8 times.

For variety find some hills and do hill repeats. Stand up out of the saddle and sprint up the hill as fast as you can, then coast down. Repeat 10 times. These are the hard sessions that every athlete dreads but they are short and highly effective. They will make you super strong and fast-track your improvement. They will get you fitter in a shorter time than going out for longer steady state rides.

Chapter 8:
Unlock the Secrets to Successful Running

Running is arguably the most technically difficult and the most demanding discipline on the body. But strangely it is the one where most people think they can just get away with it because it is seemingly easy.

According to Running USA, women are now the majority of participants in US road races. So we, as a gender, like running, and can fit it into our lifestyles.

How can I be a great runner?

The foundation of good running is aerobic capacity, running economy and lactate threshold.

Improvements in any one of these will improve your running.

Many women do not run well

This stems from a few factors:

1) Poor core muscles from too much sitting

If you think about it- even if you are active 1-2 hours a day- there is still 22-23 hours left in each day. Let's assume 8 hours sleep, 8 hours work- for most of us work involves a large proportion of sitting. Then 8 hours left for relaxing, friends, family, eating- much of this is sitting again…

So even if you are quite active at training- most people still sit down the majority of each day. This tends to weaken your core over time. If you are fresh from your "legs, bums and tums" class and have worked your core for 40 minutes- there is still a lot of time each day where the core does not have to work much at all.

Try to engage the core when you walk around the office or play with the kids and make sure when you sit- you turn your core on too.

2) **Tight hip flexors, hamstrings and calf muscles.**

These muscles get tight with sitting. Most of us are not too good at stretching. If we are tight in these muscles, the alignment of our pelvis change slightly and our body compensates in small ways to make some muscles over work and some muscles get tighter and tighter.

3) **No instruction**

Most runners have never had a coaching sessions/lesson in running. As a rule we are not "taught" how to run. We simply buy a pair of running shoes and start.

If you think about it- if we start a new sport, we would have some instruction- whether it is swimming, golf, tennis, baseball- we are shown "how" to do the activity properly.

Even people who run with a club are not often shown "how" to run but the focus is on the session- eg 4 x 400m splits

Running has lots of benefits:

- Running is one of the fastest ways to burn fat

- Running will improve your sex life and libido

- Running will help you gain great leg and bum definition

- Running decreases stress levels

- Running will strengthen your bones helping to prevent osteoporosis

- Running reduces your risk of breast and uterine cancer by 50% and cuts your risk of diabetes by 66%

- Often the winner in triathlon is that person who is the strongest runner. Sometimes the pack can stay together on the swim, the bike leaders are not too far from each other, then the one who can push ahead in the run and leave the group behind is the victor.

So learn to enjoy it but learn to do it right. If you train hard with poor running technique- you will get injured- guaranteed- it will be a matter of "when" not "if".

Increased Q Angle

Women have a wider pelvis than men. This increases the Q angle which means the knees tend to point inwards more.

Female runners are twice as likely to experience running injuries as men

This is due to anatomical differences. The most common injuries are shin splints, Achilles pain or knee pain. This changes the angle of the pull of the quadriceps. Over time this will predispose a woman to ilio-tibial band friction and mal-alignment of the patella.

Core stability training is very important for women to prevent these issues. Strength around the hip joint will also help control the movement at the hip.

A good understanding of running biomechanics is essential as well. If you do suffer with running injuries, generally it can be fixed with correct muscle strengthening and tweaking the way you run.

Where to start?

Start conservatively. If you have not run before or for a long time, start walking. This is very important if you are overweight. You are getting your joints and tendons ready for the pounding involved in running. When you are ready, add in some jogging in between.

For example, run/walk for 20 minutes. Keep building the distance but never more than 10% increase week to week.

You want to build up to running 3-4 times a week, 30-40 minutes, then add in one longer run a week if you are training for the longer distances.

Always listen to your body. If it needs an extra day off running, allow it (this does not mean skipping training. It means switch that session to swimming, cycling or a core work out!).

What about the Treadmill?

Often runners and triathletes are quite precious about "never training indoors" and hating gyms. However the treadmill does have its place!

The disadvantages are obvious:

We race outside, so we should train outside in the same conditions.

Learn to propel your body forward with your own force instead of relying on the treadmill to do it and simply try to "keep up"

The advantages are numerous:

If you are a new runner, the treadmill provides more cushioning and is easier on your joints

If you have a treadmill with a mirror in front of you- this is awesome for getting visual feedback of how your posture is when you are running and your leg and body alignment. This is invaluable. If you see a leg kicking out to the side, or your hips swinging wildly from side to side, try to make small corrections.

You can do some pretty serious hill repeats on the treadmill and get an awesome workout. You can do some fantastic speed workouts and be very objective about your speed and time. Brilliant for those wet, rainy, cold days that are unpleasant or sometimes even dangerous to go out and hit the pavements.

Of course it is not wise to do all your training indoors but once a week provides a different scene and allows you to focus on technique and form.

Proper Running Technique

I will go through some of the most important points of running so you have something to focus on and practice when you are thinking about your technique:

If possible, have someone video your gait and give you some pointers.

There are many great books written about running technique. Here I will summarize the main points of running technique which will give you a major advantage when you are training and trying to get your gait sorted.

Think about:

- Running tall
- Leaning forward slightly
- Landing on the balls of your feet. Think about hardly touching the ground. Glide!
- Minimizing upper body movement
- Relaxing your arms and shoulders
- Steady breathing
- Strong gluteal muscles
- Having a strong, stable core
- Shortening your stride length – 80% of runners over stride
- Trying not to bounce- run steady

Do not build up the mileage too quickly – no more than 10% a week.

Schedule in a combination of short interval sessions based on the principles above and longer steady state runs.

Listen to your body. If it has considerable pain, rest it for a day or two. The worst thing you can do is "push through the pain" then require 6 weeks or more off because of shin splints or some other running injury.

Strong Gluteal Muscles

This point is so important that it needs fleshing out.

The muscles in your backside are THE running muscle. The glutes are the muscles in your bottom, the muscles you sit on all day. They should be the strongest muscle in the body.

Sadly, in many runners they are the weakest. The glutes have "forgotten" what they are meant to do and other muscles compensate like the hamstrings or the lower back.

If these smaller muscles are over-working and compensating for weak, inactive glutes, this may be one reason you always get back ache when you run or always have tight hamstrings.

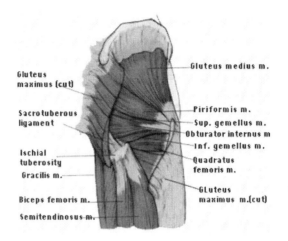

The glutes are a major hip extensor. It is from here you should be generating your power and forward momentum. The glutes also help stabilize the pelvis and keep your core solid so you do not lose energy.

Exercise:

Squats, lunges and dead lifts are the key exercises to ensuring your gluteal muscles are active, strong and ready to run. Refer to the chapter on strengthening if you are unfamiliar with these exercises.

Add these in to your program every week.

Do 3 x 12 reps. Start with body weight only, progress to dumbbells when ready.

Shoes and laces

Buying a decent pair of running shoes can be a mission! There are so many types and styles but what should you be looking for to ensure great performance and to look after your joints?

How do you know you have a good running shoe and have not just succumbed to marketing hype and become just another fashion victim?

If the shop assistant seems clueless- walk out.

If the shop assistant looks and speaks like a fellow runner- this bodes well. They might ask you about your weekly mileage, whether you pronate(tend to have flat foot) or supinate(tend to have a high arch).

Some shops will have a treadmill on site and ask you to run so they can assess your gait for themselves and hopefully advise you better on the right shoe.

Each runner is unique – so there is not "one' best running shoe or brand.

It depends on your mileage, your ability, your bio-mechanics, your previous injuries and your weight.

Here are the main things you will need to make a decision on:

1) **Weight of the shoe**

   Look for a shoe that is light. After spending all that money on ensuring your bike is as light as possible, you do not want heavy running shoes It is just extra weight you have to carry around.

2) **Motion control or neutral**

   Some shoes have anti pronation control built in if you have a tendency to roll inwards onto your arch. Many of you will know whether you do this already.

   If you have orthotics made for you from a podiatrist, I would suggest getting a neutral shoe and using the orthotic, which presumably has been made exactly for you. If the shoe store has skilled staff to analyze your running, they will be able to tell you. If they can't, and you have never had any problems or running injuries before- stick with neutral shoes unless there is a definite reason to choose something else.

3) **Amount of cushioning in the heel**

A running shoe must absorb 2-3 times your body weight on each step. Running shoes therefore place a lot of emphasis on cushioning. However, it is not simply a case of the more cushioning the better- in fact, it may be the exact opposite!

Research has shown that through the 1980s and 1990s as shoes became more and more cushioned, there was also a dramatic rise in running injuries.

Researchers studied American runners with all their technology in their shoes and compared them to primitive societies who just wore flat thin shoes with no technology and could run all day injury free!

It turned out that the thicker heel in the running shoe actually changes the gait of your running style. Runners went from landing on the ball of their foot (like primitive people) to landing on the heel (because of the large cushioning).

This set off an altered running gait and a massive increase in lower limb injuries in Western society.

As many of you may know, the pendulum has swung back to a push towards more minimal shoes with a lower heel and less "technology" as our feet were naturally designed to run and our arch was designed to cushion us.

Now I am not saying go out a get a minimalist shoe- not at all. But I would not rush out a get a super high heel with a massive cushion-as this does not allow you to run well.

If you are a new runner- you could do with some cushioning as your gait and your muscles will not have adapted much as yet. If you are an experienced runner- with no injuries- stick to what you have been doing.

If you are an experienced runner plagued with injures, perhaps it is time to look at the shoe and your gait.

As I said there is no "right" way- as everyone is at different stages, has different physical background and biomechanics. I will tell what I have done and it will be up to you to experiment for a few months with what suits your feet, your style of running.

Remember don't make any drastic changes as your muscles have to adjust slowly to any changes. Where runners get it wrong is getting excited about a new shoe or a new training method and going out and doing too much too soon. If you change your shoes- take it easy trying them out!

I always ran in traditional running shoes with 12mm heel.

I was interested in the minimalist movement as it made sense to me. I read a lot of the research. Around the same time I did a lot of work on correcting my gait- and making sure was landing on the ball of my foot instead of the heel and getting good hip extension. My running started to improve and my chronic knee injury disappeared.

When it was time to buy new shoes, I bought two pairs-a minimalist pair- that were flat 0mm and another pair 8mm heel.

I knew I could not go straight out and do the same mileage in 0mm shoes- or I would be injured within 10 days. So I used the 8mm for my "long runs" and the 0mm pair for shorter runs or treadmill runs.

As both were new shoes- I reduced my mileage a lot for a few weeks to ensure my muscles were used to the new shoes. Even so- I was aware of some new muscle aching from the 0mm shoes especially- I reduced the distance and the intensity of the runs even more.

Outcome for me: I use the 0mm for racing as they are super light and help me run faster. I have another new pair now instead of the 8mm, which are 4mm that I still use for longer runs or when I run on concrete for a bit more cushioning. I would say it takes 6 months to fully adapt to a significant change in shoe. So be careful.

So that is just my experience. I am not saying it is right or that you should do it. It depends on your feet, your fitness and your running experience. But hopefully that gives you a bit of insight into the questions you should be asking and the points you need to consider.

4) Comfort

Comfort is the most important factor when buying a shoe. Ensure there are no bits that are rubbing or causing chaffing or blisters. Consider whether you run mainly on road or off road.

You will also need to decide whether you wish to race with socks or no socks then practice this way too.

5) Laces

The last thing you want to happen is your shoe laces coming undone during a race. Time is wasted tying shoe laces and then if they come undone during the race- having to stop, break your rhythm, tie them and start again.

If you can, get speed laces or lock laces that you do not have to tie. This saves time and they do not come undone.

If you prefer to stick to conventional shoe laces- make sure you tie them in a double knot so they will not come undone.

One-piece or two-piece tri-suit?

Many of the pros wear a one-piece suit. It is more aerodynamic, more supportive, can be more flattering and your stomach is not on show.

A two-piece can be more flexible if you wear different sizes tops and bottoms. They also make for more convenient toilet stops. If you have to squat behind a bush for any reason- a one piece will find you stripping down completely!

Pacing yourself

Pacing is an important discipline in racing. Too many athletes get over-excited in a race. They start running too quickly then "blow up" and have to "shuffle" or "limp" the last few miles.

In training, get to know your comfortable steady-state pace. If possible, buy yourself a GPS watch or similar device, which will tell you what your pace is in real time. The most important metric is the average pace for the whole run. The purpose of a GPS watch or similar is as much to hold you back at the beginning of a run, as it is to keep an eye on your time.

From knowing what your pace is, you can design specific training programs.

For example you might run 10km at 8min/mile pace. So you might do an interval session 4 x 400m sprints at 6min/mile pace. This is teaching your body to run at a faster pace, training your legs to turn over faster, your breathing to adapt to this pace and your energy systems to get used to clearing out lactic acid faster and delivering you more energy.

Definitely add in one session of interval training a week to get faster quicker. It also means you have had a great workout; you are getting changes in your body without the excessive impact on your leg muscles and joints which come from long mileage runs.

Running faster

The only way to learn to run faster is to practice running faster!

Pretty obvious right?

But no! This one never fails to amaze. So many runners run their same routes at the same speed at the same time week in, week out.

And guess what?

They never improve their times from year to year.

Of course they are staying healthy and it is better than sitting on the sofa but they often get frustrated that they are putting in all this time and really seeing no results.

The secret is simple.

You MUST run faster in training.

Try interval training. There are many ways to do this.

Make sure you warm up first, then you are looking to sprint a certain distance, then recover a certain distance, then sprint then recover for a certain time period.

So an example would be sprinting to the next telegraph pole then jogging to the next one, then sprinting to the next one and so on.

If you have access to a track, a great workout is to sprint 200m, then jog 200m. Repeat 8-10 times.

Or you could do it by time. Look at your watch. Sprint 20 seconds then jog 10 seconds, sprint 20 seconds, jog 10 seconds.

Do an interval session at least once a week of 25-50 minutes and you WILL see a dramatic improvement in your time – guaranteed!

You should also enter local 5km races. These are great for developing your speed and race-experience and will also get you used to running with other people.

Hill repeats also have the same effect of improving your speed, your strength and your cardiovascular fitness in a short space of time.

Simply find a hill, run up it as fast as you can, then jog or walk back down. As you get better, increase the number of repeats and find longer and longer hills to run.

The message here is really mix it up. Do not get stuck in a routine of doing a slow plod every time you put your trainers on.

By the way hill repeats and sprints will really improve your upper body strength and your core, which is great for the longer distances. When you fatigue in the upper body or core, your running form begins to suffer and running becomes a lot harder.

Interval training means you can get a lot done in a small amount of time without spending hours and hours plodding at the same speed.

Female issues

Time of the month

"That time of the month" is inconvenient for running to say the least, but the worst time is the week before your period when the key hormone, progesterone, peaks inducing a much higher ventilation rate during exercise making a standard training session feel much harder. Do not be too hard on yourself this week. Still train of course but do an easier session if you need to.

The fluctuation in hormones can also affect your mood and make it more difficult to sleep.

Most women try to set out their training plan around this time, so they plan to have a day off or a couple of easier sessions around this time.

Do what you can to make sure you are eating well and experiment with natural foods or drinks that might help ease symptoms of pain or irritability. Some women swear by dandelion tea, ginger or cinnamon.

Sports bra

A hot sculptured body will result from many months of good training so you want to ensure all the running does not take its toll on your prized assets!
No matter what your size it is important to wear a well fitting sports bra for support when running. It should feel snug not constrictive. Look for one that stretches horizontally not vertically.
If you have small cup size, a compression type crop top is usually enough.
For larger busted women use and encapsulating style with each breast supported.
A good sports bra will be made of quick drying, breathable material so you will not be carrying around an extra pound of water.
Also look for wide shoulders with flat seaming so it does not chafe.
Replace them when you know the elastic is failing… (yes you know!)
A good idea is to change them as often as you change your trainers- every 300-400 miles or so.
Yes they might be expensive but getting breast surgery is MUCH more expensive!

Safety

When you run alone, take precautions. Do not always run the same route at the same time. Vary it up a bit.

Also let someone know when you are leaving, and when you will be back. Some people suggest running with a personal attack alarm. Also use common sense and avoid isolated areas at night.

If you wear headphones, you will be more vulnerable as you will be unable to hear an attacker approach. If you run in isolated areas it may be better not to wear head phones and stay alert.

Running during pregnancy

Should you be running at all?

There are a lot of old wives tales and myths about exercising and pregnancy. Many of them are false and for the most part, the advice is largely to do what you would normally do. If you are normally a runner- continue running.

Usually your weight or pelvic alignment will not change significantly until the third trimester yet so your gait will not have changed too much in the beginning. You should not be suffering much back pain but some women do suffer terrible morning sickness, nausea, urinary frequency and extreme fatigue. You may also experience insufficient fuel intake due to food aversions or feeling nauseous or the huge demand for nutrients of the growing baby.

Most pregnant women will be on a supplement of folic acid, iron, calcium and other pre natal vitamins to ensure the health of the mother and baby. Most experts recommend cutting down caffeine (check what is in your sports drinks- you may need to cut these out or switch them).

As the due date approaches, many women find it uncomfortable to run, so they cycle or swim instead and do walking. Most doctors advise staying active for the health of mother and baby.

It lessens stress, improves sleep, decreases back pain and lessens delivery complications and time in labor. Nutritional needs of the growing baby are still massive, so you need to pay attention that you are eating the right foods and enough foods and take extra rests when you feel tired.

How Soon Can I Return to Running After Giving Birth?

<u>0-3 weeks</u>

You probably don't feel like running yet! Check with your midwife or physical therapist about when you can think about running. For now, do walking and pelvic floor exercises.

<u>3-8 weeks</u>

It is wise to wait until your 6-week check up before doing anything more strenuous like going to the gym or running. Continue walking, pelvic floor exercises and swimming (if the bleeding has stopped).

<u>8-16 weeks</u>

Get your pelvic floor muscles assessed, see your doctor if having continued back pain, vaginal heaviness or urine loss before or during exercise. Continue building up your non impact exercise duration as intensity if you feel well.

<u>16 weeks+</u>

You should be able to return to pre-pregnancy activity levels provided you are experiencing no adverse symptoms. Remember you may feel more tired due to the demands of a new baby, breastfeeding and lack of sleep.

Give yourself time to heal and recover properly. Do not push yourself if you don't feel like it. Giving birth is a major ordeal for the body, and in some cases can be quite traumatic.

Don't think you will be back "sooner " because you are fit. The body still has to heal and recover like everyone else. Some people find it takes them 6 months before they are ready to run. Lower impact activities are usually easier to return to like cycling, swimming, yoga and walking. Focus on strengthening your core and pelvic floor.

If you are still experiencing leakage- see a pelvic floor specialist. Some specific exercise and feedback about the exercises are sometimes necessary to retrain the muscles correctly. Also your body may need more time to recover between runs- especially your pelvic floor.

Hormones

If you opt to breastfeed your hormones won't be back to normal for a year or so. This can also increase the laxity of the pelvic floor. Do not compare yourself with other women or feel bad you are not running if your friends are back sooner. Everyone's body is different and everyone's birth experience is different.

Give yourself a break, do your pelvic floor exercise's, get as much rest as the little one allows you to and make sure your nutrition is great. Good fuel will aid healing and recovery times.

Injuries

Injury tends to come as part of the running "package".

As I have said earlier, running injuries are NOT inevitable but as a result of poor technique or doing too much too soon.

More runners get injured every year than in any other sport even though it is a non contact sport. I have a whole chapter coming up on the most common running injuries and how to avoid or treat them, so this will be a reminder of the general principles to remain injury free.

Rest

Remember your rest periods – you cannot train all the time. Good running technique is important as is learning to listen to your body. The advantage of doing triathlon instead of just running is you become a much better all-round athlete.

You have more balanced muscle development and you mix up your training with other movements besides just pounding the streets.

When you are fatigued, you are more likely to get injured because your form goes. So when you feel exhausted, ease up on the distance or the intensity for a few days until you feel better.

Seriously, it is much better to have a couple of easier days training than develop shin splints or Achilles tendonitis and have to endure 6 weeks off training. This will drive you insane!

Most people think they are invincible it until they get injured. They think it won't happen to them. They keep pushing and pushing through the pain, thinking they are "different" and can "train through it" and the pain will just go away. But guess what? It doesn't!

Women are generally a bit smarter than that and tend to listen to their body a bit quicker than men.

But good training includes resting when you need to and pushing hard when you are feeling good.

Remember your physiology. You will have days when you have pushed hard, when you feel fatigued and feel "good pain". Your lungs are burning. Your legs feel heavy. You feel like you can't go on.

The process of being an athlete is pushing your body to the point where it gets tiny muscles tears (this is the muscle soreness you sometimes feel after training). The muscle then repairs itself and grows stronger. This is necessary for improvement.

Contrast this with "bad" pain. Over time, you must learn to recognize the difference and pay attention to the signs early so you can take adequate rest and prevent a teak turning into a major injury. Often "bad " pain is sharp in nature and causes you to alter your gait or your form in some way to compensate.

Also too much fatigue causes you to change your form and you should listen to this and ease up a bit. Training with bad form just reinforces poor motor patterns. You do NOT want to get stronger at the wrong thing.

This is definitely time to listen! Sometimes all you need is a couple of days off. Your body will heal and recover. You will come back stronger.

If you keep pushing at this point, your hamstring tweak will develop into a full-blown tear which means 6-8 weeks off. Or your sniffle and raised heart rate will develop into flu and glandular fever and you may need 3 months off and your season is over, gone, finished!

Learn this lesson now – do not learn the hard way.

Plan your week

In general you should not increase your training volume and intensity in the same session. Choose one. Remember to mix up your training speeds. Sometimes do long, slow runs. Sometimes choose shorter, hard intervals sessions. Do not choose hard, long runs especially in the beginning. It is not worth it.

Remember the 10% rule!

Sometimes in the beginning you can get away with it. For example if you can only run 2 miles, then increase to 4 miles. That is usually ok because the training volume is low anyway. But you would not go from running 10 miles one week, to running 8 miles, 3 times the next week because that would total 24 miles and a crazy increase of 240%. It would not be long before your body would break down with injury.

So set out a sensible training program.

Keep a training journal of how you are feeling each week.

Adjust it if you have to.

The mistake a lot of marathon runners and triathletes make is they set out their training plan but mid way through they get injured and need 3-4 weeks off. Obviously they will have missed a lot of training runs. They either jump straight back into the week they should be on or they add in extra runs trying to do all the mileage they missed according to the program and overloading their systems straight away. This is a guaranteed way to end up back on the physical therapist's couch!

Normal training pain is usually generalized by "oh my legs hurt today" rather than localized "oh there is sharp, localized pain in my knee". Definitely have a couple of days off if you experience localized pain in the same spot for more than a couple of sessions in a row.

If the pain has not gone after a couple of days rest, seek professional help. If you get it seen too quickly, the problem usually resolves itself quickly.

Essential Running Drills

There is more about running to keep in mind than just the feet! In fact, the more I learn and experience about running, the less and less it is about the feet, and the more it is about the core, the overall posture, the arms and what is going on inside your head. The feet are simply a by-product that will behave perfectly well if everything else is doing what it should be doing.

Running is a very technical sport and to get good at it, you need to break it down into its components and practice each one.

All good runners do drills – no exceptions!

It is important to get the basics right or you will start to notice niggles and injuries more frequently.

So here are a couple of easy drills that will make a big difference to your running times.

Drill 1

Most people do not bend their knee up at the back when they run. If you look at good runners they have a high knee lift at the front and at the back of their swing cycle.

This requires less distance for the leg to travel. This results in a higher cadence and less fatigue and means you will run faster.

Heel-to-butt kicks. During your normal run, begin to exaggerate knee flexion, touching the butt with the heel during each stride. Do 20 touches for both the right and left legs, then continue in your normal gait pattern.

Drill 2

Single Knee bends. Most people struggle with this one. Stand on one leg and bend your knee. Watch your knee in a mirror if possible and make sure it travels forward.

80% of people will notice either:

- They cant balance on one leg or

- Their knee drifts inwards

If either of these things happen- you will be losing energy and may be at risk of getting runner's knee due to the adverse forces at the knee joint.

The drill involves practicing this skill.

Do 3 x 15 reps twice a day.

If you think about running- it is actually a series of one knee bends done fast!

Practice this many times- this is a fundamental skill of running. If you can't balance on one leg- you will have running problems. If you cant bend your knee keeping your knee straight, you will have running problems.

Drill 3

Cadence counts. During your run, count the number of right foot strikes achieved in a span of 20 seconds. There should be 30 or more, indicating a cadence of 90 or higher. Increased cadence indicates decreased ground contact time.

Remember to stay light on your feet and think about relaxation as you run. This will reduce fatigue and make you a faster runner.

Summary

Remember to stay relaxed, stay mentally focused while you are running. Practice good form all the time.

Practice does not make perfect- Perfect practice makes perfect

Do not get stronger at the wrong thing!

Chapter 9:
Get Tough!

Mental toughness is a skill you will need in triathlon whether your event is a sprint or an Ironman. You will need it to complete your training. You will need it to train for 3 sports at once. You will need it to manage your time effectively, especially if you are fitting in work and family life as well. You will need it to balance your nutrition requirements, sleep requirements and to overcome any injuries you may pick up along the way.

You need to learn how to suffer!

Yes of course triathlon is fun but there will be days, even weeks where you just won't feel like training and your job will be to train anyway!

As well as training your body for the event, equally you are training your mind. You must practice perseverance everyday when you are out training in the bad weather, when you ride or run further than you have ever gone before, when you are in pain but must push through the pain barrier.

Most coaches ignore this aspect of training, which is a mistake.

Most books on triathlon also ignore the mental training you must do to succeed.

So you have done very well to buy this book and to read this far!

Without this mental strength and skill, you may as well give up.

It is so important.

Mental attitude and mental strength is something you need to practice from the very beginning, get better at as you improve and get up to race standard. By the way, this improved mental strength will carry over into your normal life. You will notice huge improvements here too.

You need to practice not quitting during training.

You need to practice not quitting in the race when your body wants to give up.

You need to practice digging deep and see what you are really made of.

Mental toughness is easy to get: you simply decide to have it.

You decide to get out and train when you don't feel 100 per cent.

You decide not to quit during the race no matter how badly you feel and

You decide to dig deeper and pass a few people at the end of a race.

It sounds easy but mental toughness alone isn't good enough. You need to combine that mental toughness with self-awareness and intelligence. You could decide to train hard every day and be tough enough to do it. However, after about 10 days you would be burnt out and would have trouble finishing the race.

You need to know when to apply that mental toughness you simply decided to have.

Say you are running your first half marathon. Everyone goes off very quickly at the start. Do you dig deeper and keep up with them? No, that would be stupidity. You need to have enough discipline to keep to your own pace. The ability to push yourself cannot go deeper than your physical ability.

Towards the end of the race when your legs feel as though they are falling off and all you want to do is stop, this is when you apply that toughness. You keep going and hold your cadence and concentrate on your breathing and on good technique.

What if you see a fellow competitor up ahead who you know you have beaten before?

Do you let her win?

Not a chance!

You are in a race, sister, and you do not give up for a second until you cross the finish line.

Fitness, confidence, toughness, self-awareness, intelligence and, most importantly, discipline are what you need to be a successful endurance athlete. Everything has to come together. It's not easy for anyone. Mental strength must be practiced and developed.

You need to go into a race or a training session with the attitude that you are there to do well and to do your very best.

Get some family or friends to support you and give you encouragement. Also do not be intimidated by all the "bling" on display. Many women get discouraged, intimidated or put off by all the fancy gear, all the expensive bikes and all the testosterone on show when they turn up to an event.

Do not worry! Two things: many of the people on expensive bikes do not know how to ride them – they are slow beginners who just happen to have a bit of cash.

The other thing is if there are a lot of men around showing off remember that you are NOT racing them! So this is irrelevant. You are in your own race, with women in your own age group so keep it all in perspective.

Focus on yourself. Focus on your preparation and focus on enjoying the day.

Being nervous

Guess what? On race day everyone will be nervous, whether it is their first event or they are seasoned pros! Use that energy to give you power.

To keep nerves under control, preparation is key. You have done your training.

You have done your pre-race rehearsal. You know where T1 and T2 are.

You have sufficient nutrition and so on.

Remember everyone is in the same boat. Do a pre-race warm-up to spin the legs and get in the zone. And remember to breathe!

Find some motivational sayings or a mantra you can say to yourself over and over to help you focus on how good you are feeling, how strong you are, how much you are going to enjoy the race.

Even during the race you may have to battle fragile mental or emotional states like boredom, fear, fatigue or self-doubt. Be prepared for this and banish these thoughts from your mind immediately.

Fill your mind constantly with positive, strong thoughts and allow nothing else to enter your head

Here are 2 tools you can use:

Self Talk

An average person has 60,000 thoughts per day, most of them are negative! For example "I'm hopeless at this sport", "why am I bothering?" and so on.

"Extensive research in the sports psychology world confirms that an athlete's internal dialogue significantly influences performance" Seltz 2009

It doesn't matter what happens in the race like a bad swim, focus on the present and what you can do well **right now** to improve things. Often this negative self-talk is just a bad habit.

You need to practice filling your mind up with positive thoughts. For example, celebrate every mile you have completed. Tell yourself you are enjoying it. Tell yourself you are looking forward to the bike, to the run.

You need to practice it in training and on race day. Make it a new habit.

Visualization

Visualization is seeing in your mind a perfect video of you succeeding. For example you completing the perfect swimming stroke, enjoying it, feeling strong and coming out of the water in the front of the pack; you completing a quick transition, you crossing the finish line confident and with a smile on your face.

Practice visualizing these scenarios for 1 minute before you go to bed. Try to make it as real as possible. Feel the sun on your back and the wind on your hair. Try to hear the noise of the crowd, the loud speaker and the other competitors.

See yourself managing pressure and stress calmly and in control.

Practice these tools daily and you will find you approach the race with excitement instead of nerves and with eager anticipation instead of dread!

Make sure all throughout your training, you do mental rehearsal and mental training.

This step is key to make sure you have run through the race many times before hand in your mind.

At least for 10 minutes, 3 times a week, sit down somewhere quiet and visualize race day. Visualize arriving at the venue and watching lots of people rushing around.

Visualize everything as vividly as you can,- the sights, the smells, the sounds.

Listen to the loudspeaker barking instructions, visualize yourself feeling confident and calm.

Visualize yourself arriving having everything you need. Watch yourself racking your bike and setting up your transition area.

Visualize yourself rehearsing the transition entrances and exits,

Visualize yourself having your last portion of fuel before zipping up your wetsuit- still feeling excited but calm and confident.

Visualize the gun going and completing the perfect swim, an easy transition, cycling well, coming back in good time.

Visualize T2 going well, and completing the run in a personal record and crossing the line to many cheers and applause, thrilled with your time and having had a fantastic race.

Visualization is also very important for every training session to help perfect your technique as quickly as possible.

This does not need to take long. Do it 2 minutes before you drift off to sleep. Do it while waiting at a red traffic light or waiting in a queue or for the kettle to boil.

See in your mind a perfect video of you swimming perfectly. For example visualize your elbow coming out of the water, your fingertips entering the water in front of your shoulder. Visualize the strong pull through, your horizontal body position, your easy breathing manner and your powerful kick.

Visualize enjoying it, feeling strong and coming out of the water in the front of the pack.

Try to make it as real as possible. Feel the sun on your back and the water pressure as you pull through. Try to smell the chlorine or the sea salt. See yourself managing pressure and staying confident and in control. Picture the perfect stroke, the perfect cycle and the perfect run.

Also while you are doing your training, practice your perfect technique, and practice filling your mind with positive thoughts. Of course training is tough most of the time- but try not to focus on the pain.

Instead fill your mind with thoughts like:

"Its great to be out here in the fresh air"

"I'm getting stronger and stronger"

"I can't wait for the race"

"I am always confident and in control"

"The more it hurts, the better I get"

When any negative thought enters your head- banish it immediately!

Pick one or two mantras that resonate with you and say them over and over with feeling to give you strength when you experience self-doubt or fatigue or feel like giving up.

That is the time to shout the mantra in your head and get back on track!

Practice these tools daily and you will find you approach the race with excitement instead of nerves and with eager anticipation instead of dread!

Goal Setting

You may be peaking for your big race of the year but make sure you set mini goals along the way. This keeps you on track but it also gives you mini celebrations along the way, which are really important.

You are putting in a lot of time training and it is important that you observe that you are improving and achieving the whole way along not just on race day.

Make the goals specific and measurable.

For example at the start of the year- maybe you could run 5km in 29.38mins.

Your goal would NOT be simply "to get faster" but it should be something specific like:

"I will run 5 km in 25 minutes by December 1st."

You might have a series of mini goals along the way to culminate in the race.

For example if you had booked a half Ironman, maybe you also book a couple of sprint distance triathlons, a couple of Olympic distance races and a 60-mile cycle sportive.

These will all give you race practice, packing your race bags, testing your nutrition and hydration and practicing your transitions.

Race experience is very valuable. If you are training for a triathlon, participating in swim only events or 5km/10km runs really helps with the whole racing experience. It also helps you to see what your body can do in a race. Often you will be surprised and produce results you never thought possible in training.

Summary

Many triathletes pay lip service to mental training. But very few actually schedule some practice. It is so important that all the pros from every sport hire a mind coach to truly engage the power of the brain. Anyone who does this wishes they started earlier.

If you actually do this a couple of times a week- you will reap fantastic rewards and all your training will be more productive!

Chapter 10: Transitioning Like a Pro

Transition is where you change from one discipline to another in a triathlon.

It is a key area where you can gain a massive advantage over your competitors. So if you read this chapter and implement it, you will leave a lot of the field behind you.

Transition 1 (T1) is the transition from swim to bike and transition 2 (T2) is from bike to run. Transition is the one area most beginners never practice.

Most beginners turn up on race day never having thought about the transitions. Some women have been spotted checking their makeup and combing their hair after the swim, thinking that the time clock stopped during transition!

You can be sure the clock does not stop and every minute counts. There is not much point setting the alarm for 5am each morning to swim before work to improve 1 minute over the season to then waste 3 minutes in transition trying to find kit that should be out, easy to find and ready to go!

Spend some time to think about your kit lay out for a fast transition and practice your routine so that on race day when you are puffing, panting and the adrenalin is pumping, you will know exactly what to do and where everything is.

As with most things preparation and practice is essential. Some women do think about it the night before and do a quick run through, but I suggest preparing earlier than that.

Race day is full of adrenalin, nerves and stress, lots of competitors rushing around and lots of marshals shouting instructions. So your transition plan should be automatic, well practiced so you could do it in your sleep.

The other risk when you get stressed and are in a rush, is that you do silly things that you never normally do. One big risk in transition is getting disqualified. It is easy to grab your bike without putting your helmet on first or unbuckling the chin-strap as you ride back towards T2. Be careful.

Practice these things at home each week. When you return from a long ride, also do not undo your chin-strap and helmet until your bike is secure in its place.

If you take it off early at home- you risk doing this in transition.

What if the night before, you find you have forgotten something, or run out of your favorite gel? Or don't have two spare inner tubes? The shops are closed and you will arrive at the race stressed!

Also it is a great idea to practice your transitions once a week, the whole way through training. Most women start this run through practice in race week (if at all!)

Sure- this is better than not doing it at all- but the best way is to plan your bike session to be followed by a short run. Lay out your gear for the run for when you get back from the bike ride. Keep the clock ticking and quickly change and be out the door on the run.

Make sure you develop a routine so you do the same thing every time in the same order.

Arriving at Transition

When arriving in the transition area on race day, first rack and secure your bike. This seems obvious but at every event, somebody's bike falls off the rack damaging it or a neighboring bike. Not cool!

Next, place a large towel on the ground next to your bike. Take out your race belt with race number for the bike and run and place your bike shoes on top of your race number. This stops the race number blowing away.

Another way of doing this is to put your race belt under your wet suit so you don't have to worry about it or put it on in transition, however don't try this for the first time on race day. Some competitors will safety pin their race number on their shirt, but if it starts flapping on the bike it can be very irritating, so it is wise to choose to use a race belt. Race belts can be purchased for about three dollars from most stores that stock tri gear.

Make sure that the tongue of your shoes and laces are open to make it as easy as possible to get your feet in and out.

Place your bike shoes on the towel directly behind your running shoes. Loosen up the straps and make sure they are open and ready to place your feet in them. Most of the time, competitors don't wear socks with shoes on the bike or the run to save time.

Leave the portion of the towel closest to you when you arrive open to stand on. The reason you do this is because, as you exit the swim and come into the transition area, you will have dirt, sand, grass and small rocks on your feet. Wipe your feet as you arrive. Also place a water bottle near this area so that you can wash away any debris you pick up.

You should have your hydration for the bike already loaded in the bike cages but you should have some extra water bottles in transition ready as back up. You might need a quick sip in transition or you might need to simply pour it on your head after the bike to cool you off.

Place your helmet on your bike bars and put your shades (if you are going to wear some) inside. This serves as a reminder to put your helmet on before you leave the transition area.

After you are set, run through everything mentally to double-check and make sure that you haven't forgotten anything.

Some other things to remember are:

- Reset your bike computer
- Double-check to make sure your bike is in the right gear (you need to be on your small chain ring in front and a gear that you can easily push coming out of Transition One).

Many women new to triathlon see the transition area as a place to regroup, rest, chat and get their gear together. WRONG!

This is a place where you can gain serious advantage over your competitors.

It really is the 4th discipline of triathlon and needs to be thought about, planned and practiced. The clock does not stop while you are in there, every second extra adds to your race time!

Remember you can more easily and quickly knock 2 minutes off your transition time than 2 minutes off you swim time!

You need to make it efficient, easy and effective so you use the least amount of energy possible and do not get stressed and flustered.

Race rules mean you must ALWAYS have your helmet on in transition

Do not start cycling without your helmet on. Do not even run with your bike until you have your helmet on. You may be instantly disqualified. Marshalls take this very seriously. Put your helmet on your bike.

When you come back off the bike leg into T2, make sure you keep your helmet on until the bike is securely racked in its correct spot.

Practice your plan

Think about the most efficient way to move from swim to bike (T1) and bike to run (T2). Practice it lots of times physically and also rehearse it lots of times mentally. By the time race day comes you should be on autopilot.

Be as minimalist as possible. Get rid of any steps you don't need, like socks or gloves.

Get in and out fast!

De-clutter your transition.

At least once a week- when you plan a ride, also plan to come back and run straight away so you are practicing the transition as well.

Think about what you need and set it up so when you come back you keep your watch on, rack your bike, helmet off, sun hat on, change your shoes, grab an extra gel if you need one or a sip of water and head straight off.

Over the course of a few months write down what you need and start to create a list of what you need for race day, what gels suit you, how much water you need for the run- depending on your distance, if you need a hat and sun glasses, if you prefer the same bike socks and run socks, if you prefer to change socks, or if you prefer no socks.

It is important to sort out all these things along the way.

Also make sure you do them systematically, in the same order, each and every time

So when you come home with the bike, take off your helmet, bike shoes in the same way and put on your run shoes and socks, sun hat and whatever other change you are making in the same way.

Do it the same every time!

Race a Friend

A truly great way to simulate race day if you have a friend also training for triathlon or with your tri club is to set up a transition practice mini circuit.

So you might be dressed in your wetsuit. Set your stopwatch and shout go!

Both run to a tree or a cone(eg 50m away) and back, then quickly change into cycle gear and run to the tree/cone again and back then quickly change into run gear.

The competition of racing each other plus the stop watch will certainly focus the mind and will show up some weaknesses that you don't tend to see when you are by yourself

Getting Through T1 Fast

The first challenge in coming into T1 is locating your bike.

Have you ever returned to a car park and had trouble finding your car? You can have a similar experience in a large transition area. Note carefully where your rack spot is and how to find it from the swim exit and bike entrance.

From your rack, know where the bike and run exits are and the quickest route to them. On race day when you return to T1 after the swim, some competitors may already be gone so the whole bike rack area will look completely different!

Try using a bright, distinctive towel to help in spotting your area. You should also pick a landmark like 3rd row back in line with the flagpole (for example).

The next challenge in T1 can be getting out of the wet wetsuit!

This is something no one tells you. I remember clearly that it was not something I practiced in my first race. I had borrowed a wet suit from a friend. I tried it on when it was dry, and took it off- no problem I thought- it fits perfectly. I never did one training session in it or tried to get it off when it was wet until race day!

Whoops! (I'm sure you can see where this is going!)

So race day came, I felt good. I did the swim, and came out of the water with the leaders- so far, so good! I was surprised to find I was dizzy getting out of the water- that's strange I thought- I had swum far further than that in training.

Oh well so I slowed down a bit, found my bike then tried to get the wetsuit off. I was still dizzy and it was extremely difficult. I eventually had to sit down and struggle to get it off my ankles. By this stage I had lost the leaders and my heart rate was sky high!

Needless to say I bought my own wetsuit thereafter and practiced getting it off regularly!

Start the swim with your full bike/run outfit under your wetsuit. A one or two-piece tri-suit is ideal. Any clothing changes will add lots of time.

Next step is helmet on and grabbing your gear for the bike. Most of it should be on your bike already.

If you have decided to go with bike shoes, the fastest way through T1 is to leave them in the pedals. You can fix them in place with rubber bands so they are easy to put on. As you as you start pedaling they will easily snap. Starting with them on the bike, will get you going much quicker than others who are sitting down putting on their shoes.

You run with your bike to the mounting area, then hop on the bike and start pedaling with your feet on top of the shoes until you get to cruising speed then slip your feet into the shoes. Keep your eyes on the road at all times, not on your feet.

You will have gained good time on other athletes. This is not really a beginner's technique but if you are feeling confident and keen, try it many times in practice!!

If you are a beginner, you can do your first couple of triathlons with running shoes on and clip-in pedals on your bike so you do not have to change shoes. This is fine and will save time.

Everything you need on the bike course should be attached to your bike. Gels or food should be taped to the bike. Water bottles should already be on board, sunglasses looped to a cable, spare tube in a seat pack and a CO_2 cartridge taped to the seat post.

Making T2 Child's Play

When coming back from the bike into T2, slip your feet out of the shoes as you approach T2. Keep pedaling and then, before the line, swing your leg over so you can run straight away into transition. Practice this many times beforehand so you are confident.

If you are not confident or it is your first race simply slow the bike down to a stop and get off the bike safely.

In T2, keep your helmet on until you have racked the bike. Practice running with your bike while holding the seat in a quiet parking lot or a quiet road. People do fall over in transition or crash into other athletes when their handlebars fly off in a different direction!

Tying your running-shoe laces in a bow takes time. Eliminate this step using lace locks or speed laces. To help your feet slide smoothly into your running shoes, prime them with a sprinkling of baby powder.

In T2, grab what you need and go. Put on your hat and fuel belt (most race belts have a place for a few gels) while you are running. It is always faster to complete your tasks moving down the course rather than standing in front of your rack.

Mental Rehearsal

The transition area is a frenzy of activity, chaotic and busy. The sooner you are in and out the better. Do lots of mental rehearsal. Picture yourself at every stage: what do you need?

Plenty of mental rehearsal and physical rehearsal will ensure you have not forgotten anything. Part of the stress of the night before and on race day is the certainty you have forgotten something! I know one athlete who had prepared everything with meticulous detail, arrived at the race and realized she had forgotten to bring her bike!!!

At the race it is a really good idea to do a walk through. So rack your bike, lay everything out meticulously at your transition area then do a walk through. Walk over to where you will exit the swim, then walk the exact path you will take you get to your bike.

Picture what it will look like with everyone's bikes there and lots of people rushing around. Picture yourself doing your quick change from swim gear to bike gear effortlessly.

Then walk from the bike to the T1 exit so you know exactly where it is and the path you will take. Then walk from the T2 entrance back to your bike, picture yourself doing the quick change into running gear and walk to the T2 exit. Then find where the finish line is so there is no confusion at the end.

This exercise will only take 5-10 minutes but will save you masses of time if you get it wrong. I have seen this at races many times where the athlete heads off quickly towards the wrong exit then has to double back.

Mental rehearsal is also something you can do for 5 minutes here and there throughout your week. It helps lay down strong neural pathways helps your brain remember the sequence. When you picture things vividly, the brain can't distinguish between reality and vivid mental rehearsal. Transition is a brilliant thing to picture mentally for 5 minutes each day.

Picture every detail as vividly as possible.

When you do this the first time, have a piece of paper nearby to write everything down you need, in two columns for T1 and T2.

As you get more familiar with it- you should not need to write much- only add the occasional thing that you may have forgotten.

Check your race list many times and laminate it.

I have known people to get to a race and forget their wetsuit, their bike or their ID.

(Not the same person I hasten to add) But it is easy to do.

So prepare this stage thoroughly.

Do not simply pray and hope it be OK on the day.

Make sure of it!

Brick Sessions

An important phrase you will need to know when doing triathlon training is "brick sessions". Training in one sport then moving to another straight away is called a brick session – often bike then run (mainly because your legs feel like bricks when you start to run!).

The blood flow needs to change from your cycling muscles to your running muscles. Sometimes you feel like your legs are wobbly. Sometimes they feel very heavy. This is normal. Don't worry but you do need to practice it. The more you do it, the better you will be.

Brick sessions refer to training two disciplines back to back during the same workout. Bricks are a very important part of triathlon training and they are sometimes overlooked. The two disciplines should be trained one after the other with minimal or no interruption in between, just as you would do in a race.

Many people do not train like this and do a few token bricks in race week or not at all.

However one of the biggest keys to triathlon is switching between sports quickly and efficiently.

Brick training will help you:

- Master transitions (as I have discussed above)

- Teach your legs to run straight after a bike without feeling like jelly

- Train your mind to cope with a new sport at high

intensity

- Progress faster than your competitors, many of whom will not bother to do brick training

It is NOT enough just to train the three sports separately throughout the week- they MUST be put together and trained back to back. Not every workout, of course, but at least once a week. Also do not freak out and think you need to do a full bike then a full run.

Part of the art of triathlon is learning to pace yourself in the swim and the bike leg so you have enough endurance and energy left for the run.

Even very strong runners often get this wrong and find themselves really suffering on the run and posting terrible times. If you are not good at pacing, buy yourself a heart rate monitor and stick to a decent aerobic pace, which you have practiced staying at for the duration of your event.

The idea is to mix it up a bit.

So you may do a medium bike and a short run.

Or a full swim and a medium bike

Or many other combinations in between.

Brick sessions may refer to a bike/run workout, a swim/bike workout or even a run/bike workout (if you are training for a duathlon).

Many people ignore these knowing it is something they "should" do, but if they do not schedule it in their plan, it simply never gets done!

Chrissie Wellington, four time World Ironman champion, credits brick sessions as THE most important session of her week! She did brick sessions EVERY week.

She acknowledged that she was not the fastest individual swimmer, cyclist or runner.

At any one sport she would have been beaten, but put them all together and she was the best.

So schedule it and do it!

It does not always have to take a massive amount more time!

If the major focus of your day is to get a 40-mile bike in, focus on that and you may choose to do a quick 15-minute run on the end. You don't always have to follow with a 10 -20 km run! You are just trying to teach your body to be able to run after a decent bike ride.

Brick sessions will teach you so much:

- Your legs to run well off the bike

- Give you mental confidence

- Reduce the risk of "jelly" legs

- Give you physical confidence and certainty that you can do it well as you will have done it so many times

- Help you identify the correct nutrition for you- so you don't risk stomach cramps on the run through too much fluid or incorrect fuel on the bike

- Help you master transitions- as you practice your bike-run routine or swim-bike routine

- Reduce risk of leg cramps

- Help you understand the perfect pacing for your bike leg so you have enough "left in the tank" for the run

Swim/bike brick

While you are swimming a lot of the blood will be in your shoulders and arms so when you stand up on land, the blood tends to rush towards your legs, causing you to feel faint or giddy.

So start kicking your legs hard for the last 50-100meters of the swim to get the blood in the legs so you are not stumbling around or have to sit down for a minute until you get your bearings.

A swim/bike workout that simulates race conditions will help you minimize this problem.

Always start your bike portion using an easier gear than the one you plan on using during the main part of the race. This will give your legs a chance to get used to the new sport and accumulate less lactic acid than they would if you started from the beginning with a tough gear.

Logistically, some people train at a pool and can have the bike chained up outside.

Other people train at a gym pool where they can go quickly inside and jump on a spin bike or turbo trainer set up by the pool.

Obviously if you have the chance to swim in open water with a wetsuit, do this to practice the transition specifically (and getting out of a wet wetsuit!).

Here are some example swim/bike brick sessions:

Sprint distance: 200 meter swim and 15 minute bike at 80-90% max heart rate (MHR)

Olympic: 400 meter swim followed by 25 minute bike at 80% MHR

Half Ironman: 2000 meter swim followed by 2 hour bike ride at 80% MHR

Ironman: 3000-4000 meter swim followed by 2-3 hour bike ride at 75% MHR

These are just guidelines workouts.

Sometimes you won't have time to do these longer sessions, but even if you can do one of the disciplines properly then bolt on 10-15 minutes of the second discipline- you will get valuable transition practice in and continue to remind the body that there will be something more to come.

Little and often is much better than doing it all at once the week before the event!

You can also add in repeats for variety such as:

3 x (500 meter swim + 5 mile bike).

This is more useful and time-efficient than doing a 1,500 meter swim followed by a 15 mile bike, because you will switch sports 6 times instead of only once.

Bike/run bricks

These are more important mainly because the transition between bike and run is the tougher of the two during a triathlon. There are two reasons for this

1) You are using largely similar muscle groups

2) You are already a long way through the race so will already be exhausted and energy depleted!

Most people's recount of their brick workouts consist of a medium/long bike ride followed by a medium run. Be careful not to train at "medium" the whole time.

You definitely want to make sure you do some very hard sessions or you will not have the top end speed when you need it in a race.

Although these kinds of bricks are great, other recommendations are a sequence of short/medium rides alternated with a series of short runs.

Here are a couple of bike/run examples:

Sprint triathlon workout: 5-6 mile bike + 1mile run at 75% MHR - repeat three or four times.

Or

Try this one: a 15 minute cycle at the hardest threshold you can maintain followed by a 10 minute run (5 minutes at threshold and 5 minute sprint with anything you have left)

Olympic triathlon workout: 70 minute bike followed by a 45 minute run at 75% MHR

Or

Strength brick: Cycle a 30 minute hilly course or hill repeats, followed by 10 minute running hill repeats.

By doing a series of short repeats you also switch sports (and therefore muscles used) several times in the same workout. You are teaching your legs and body to switch as fast as possible and as efficiently as possible between two very different kinds of effort.

Again, consider a series of short repeats. These are very efficient especially when you are short on time.

Ironman or half ironman distance: 60 minute cycle followed by 90 minute run.

It may be difficult to fit this in every week if you already do a long run and a long ride. If you are struggling for time- switch this for your long run.

It is more important to learn to run with bike fatigue in the legs.

As race day approaches you may want to put all three together.

1000m hard swim followed by a 5km 90% MHR cycle followed by a 3km 90% MHR run.

(Increase the distances for the Ironman!)

If you have never done a brick before, you should get used to them gently before attempting the kind of workouts described above.

Start with a 1-mile jog or jog/walk after every bike ride. You can start by walking briskly when you get off the bike and them move to a jog or run within ¼ to ½ mile.

You can also attempt your first brick by biking in the morning and then running in the afternoon or after a 1 to 2 hour break.

When you stop biking and start running the legs may feel "strange" and heavy and the heart rate goes up as the body tries to switch the blood from flowing into the muscles used for cycling to those used for running.

This feeling is more pronounced at the start of the run and usually the legs get better as time passes - although probably never as fresh as those you have when you run without biking beforehand.

Brick workouts help shorten the time your legs take to adapt thus allowing you to run better and faster. It is not uncommon to experience cramps when starting to run after biking, especially if you are not used to it.

As usual, listen to your body and slow down if you feel a cramp coming. Gel and water will also help if you are experiencing cramps due to the decrease in muscle fuel.

Summary

Transition practice and brick training are secrets the pros use every week to give them the edge. They will get you the quickest results and make any race you enter so much less stressful.

They do not have to take much time. Do not ignore them!

Chapter 11:

The 5 Most Common Triathlon Injuries

Triathlon is a non contact sport.

That would imply that there should be very few injuries unlike basketball, netball or hockey where collisions and contact frequently occur. Also the stop/start nature of netball, basketball, and hockey gives rise to twisting injuries fairly often. Triathlon does not have this risk factor either.

However triathletes do find themselves on the treatment table a little too often!

Overuse accounts for over 80 percent of all triathlon injuries according to a sample of surveys conducted by Universities in USA, UK and Australia. In other words- doing too much, too soon.

Also poor biomechanics is a huge factor in sustaining injuries. Biomechanics is the way we perform an activity-our technique. Other injuries come from collisions with cars, collisions with other athletes and miscellaneous.

Running produces the highest number of injuries of the three disciplines. It is highly technical, many people get no instruction in "how" to run and there is 3 times your bodyweight pounding through each leg each time your foot hits the ground.

It is a recipe for disaster!

One of the great things about triathlon training is that even if you can't run for a few weeks, you can still bike, swim and strength train. However ideally, follow your program, listen to your body and avoid the injury in the first place!

It is heart breaking to train all season and peak for your big race, only to be faced with pulling out with an injury before you even toe the start line. Many athletes face this agonizing decision- but by training smarter- you can make sure this does not happen to you.

Most of these injuries are avoidable…

Triathletes can be an obsessive bunch though, so over use injuries are common, pushing through the pain, pushing the mileage too quickly and not bothering learning technique are major risk factors for getting injured.

Injuries are much easier to prevent than treat

Often a couple of days off may prevent a niggle from becoming a full-blown injury that may take 6 weeks to treat. So, follow your training program, schedule some rest days, listen to your body and avoid the injury in the first place!

Here are the top 5 injuries, that triathletes suffer, how to prevent them and treat them if they do appear.

Iliotibial (IT) Band Syndrome

This is the curse of runners across the globe! You will feel sharp pain on the outside of the knee joint. If you keep running through it, the pain gets worse and worse until it completely debilitates you until you are even limping when you walk.

Sometimes cyclists will experience it too but the majority of sufferers are runners.

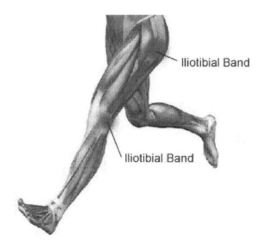

The IT band is a band of tissue that stretches from the hip to the knee down the outside of your leg. It gets aggravated by repetitive bending at the knee when you run, causing friction and inflammation at the knee joint.

It can flare up due to increasing mileage too quickly or due to poor running and cycling technique. Another major cause is weak gluteal muscles.

To treat it

- Rest from running or cycling
- Get a sports massage on your IT band to loosen it off

- Spend some time in the gym strengthening your gluteal muscles. Try exercises like squats, walking lunges and one-leg lunges, keeping your pelvis stable. Weak hip muscles is a primary cause of ITB pain. Most of us do have weak hips as the majority of our day is spent sitting.

- If you get chronic IT band symptoms, buy a foam roller and roll on it every night after running to keep the IT band loose.

- If it does not ease off in 2-3 weeks with the above suggestions, you should consider having a sports physical therapist look at your gait, your running technique, your feet, and your shoes. It will be something slightly amiss in your alignment. Even a few millimeters of internal rotation at the hip or drop in the arch of the foot can trigger this knee pain.

- Also note that the more mileage you do, the closer to perfect your technique needs to become. So whilst you may have got away with running 5 km twice a week last year, if you have ramped up the mileage to 4 times a week running 8-15 miles this year-you may be at risk of ITB pain. Make sure your knee does not roll inwards as you land....

- Sometimes a friend who runs behind you can check this, but get professional advice quickly if this does not ease up by itself – because this condition DOES NOT go away if you do not improve your strength and your gait.

Achilles Tendonitis

You will feel pain at your Achilles tendon. This is the tendon just above your heel bone.

If you squeeze it, you will feel pain. It may look red or feel like there is a bump on it.

Often sufferers describe extreme pain when they get out of bed in the morning then it eases off as they get going and warm up. Sometimes it is very painful at the beginning of a run then eases during the run.

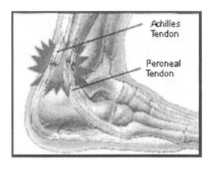

Do not ignore the pain, even if you can run through it. It will get worse! If it becomes chronic, you may have pain for 3-6 months or longer.

This injury can occur due to increasing the mileage too soon, tight calf muscles, or poor running technique for example over-pronation when your foot lands when running.

To treat it:

• Get a sports massage to loosen off the calf muscles

and get some increased blood flow in the Achilles tendon

- Stop running for a few weeks.
- Focus on calf stretches
- Get a professional to look at your running technique and see if there are any improvements to be made
- Strengthening the calf muscles can help – do calf raises 3 sets 15 resp. Do them on the edge of a step so you can drop your heel below the horizontal and get full range.

Patellar Tendonitis

You will feel pain in the center of your knee, almost right under the kneecap. You will feel it when cycling, running or walking up and down steps.

It usually happens due to tight quadriceps, the muscles the run down the front of your thigh. This pulls the kneecap against the thigh bone (femur). It can also happen due to poor bike fit or poor cycling technique. Sometimes it happens simply due to increasing bike mileage too quickly.

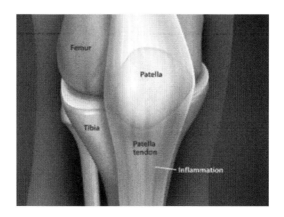

To treat it:

- If you have not had a bike fit done, book one
- Stretch your quadriceps
- Have a few weeks off the bike

- Strengthen your quadriceps- lunges and squats help

- Avoid doubling up on a hilly bike session, with a heavy leg weights session. Ensure adequate rest if you start to feel a twinge in this area

Stress Fractures

You will feel pain in the bone during running; mainly it occurs in the shin-bone. Sometimes you will feel it in the foot.

It usually occurs due to increasing the mileage too quickly. The constant pounding without sufficient rest produces tiny micro fractures in the bone.

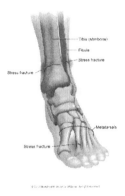

To treat it:

•   Rest from running – at least 6-8 weeks

•   If it has not gone completely, get an x-ray to confirm it but even then the cure is more rest!

•   Do intermittent treadmill training to take away some of the pounding

•   Do strength training and high intensity interval training as suggested in the running chapter so you do not have to do excessive long slow miles

If you do get a stress fracture, do not be a hero and try to come back too quickly. You got the stress fracture from doing too much! So do not come back and repeat the same mistake. I know of people who have required a full year off running.

As you begin your comeback do more cross trainer, rowing machine and bike to get your leg strength and cardio back without the pounding. Also get a gait analysis as well to ensure your running style is not placing excessive torsional force through the legs.

So listen to your body! Prevent most of these injuries by not increasing the mileage too quickly.

Rotator Cuff Tendonitis/Shoulder Pain

You notice a pain in your shoulder when your arm is extended above your head during the freestyle, front crawl stroke. It could feel like a dull pain or a sharp pain or a pinch.

It occurs due to muscle imbalance around the shoulder. Front crawl/freestyle develops the front of the shoulder and the chest muscles more than the back of the shoulder.

It also occurs due to poor technique. The rotator cuff tendons become pinched and trapped when the arm rises above the head. When this repeatedly occurs- ie swimming training- inflammation and swelling occur and you will experience pain. If you continue to push through the pain, it is possible a full thickness tear of the tendon may occur.

Do not build up to lots of mileage if you do not come from a swimming background or you do not have good swimming form. Do make the time and the investment to take some lessons.

Do the drills.

Do the practice slowly at first then follow up and get more feedback.

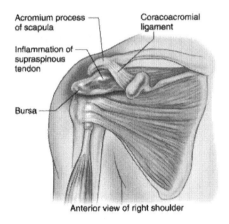

Anterior view of right shoulder

Some people try to take the cheap way out and buy a swim DVD or read a book on swim technique. This is certainly helpful but you do need feedback from a qualified swim coach who can check your technique and make corrections. Whilst you think you look like the next Missy Franklin, you most probably are very far from it.

Swimming is one of the most technical disciplines. In my view some lessons are imperative.

Also from a racing point of view, good swim technique is important for gaining the quickest time with the most efficiency. Poor swimmers come of out the water completely exhausted because they have spent the time thrashing about in the water getting nowhere fast.

They have used so much energy they can barely get their wetsuit off and then spend the first half of the bike leg recovering.

Fast swimming does not come from big muscles, it comes from good technique.

To treat it:

- Stop swimming for a few weeks
- Get some sports massage on the tight shoulder muscles
- Stretch your chest and the front of your shoulder regularly
- Book some lessons to look at your technique
- Spend some time in the gym strengthening your posterior rotator cuff and rear deltoids. Use light weights or resistance bands. Ask a personal trainer in the gym to check your technique during the exercises as well. When you return to the pool, start slow and focus on your technique.

Most of these injuries are preventable. Remember good technique for all disciplines and build up mileage gradually.

Also notice how important strength training is to prevent most injuries.

Make sure you have added strength training to your weekly program.

Signs of Overtraining

Too much mileage without enough recovery will not only lead to niggles and serious injuries, it will also result in decreased performance. You will become frustrated by training as hard as you can while noticing worse and worse performances.

It takes many athletes years and years to learn that your body strengthens during recovery

During exercise, your body is under stress. Your body is suffering micro tears and trauma in the muscles and bones. It is during rest and recovery that you get faster and stronger.

You will notice sleep patterns being disturbed and energy levels suffering. You may notice you are a bit grouchy and irritable. If it continues for a time, your appetite will suffer and your immune system will crash. You will get ill and your body will force you to take a rest.

It does not just happen to ironman athletes during huge mileage. Recreational athletes suffer as well. We have to balance deadlines, work, chores, kids, bills as well.

It does not take much to overload the system.

Signs of overtraining:

- **Dehydration**. Just a 2% drop in hydration can

decrease your performance massively. It can take a few days of concentrated hydration to recover.

• **Poor sleep**. Consistent poor sleep results in a decrease of growth hormone. This is necessary for rebuilding muscle fibers. Poor sleep also decreases immune function, reaction time and energy levels. Sometimes overtraining stresses the nervous system and hormonal system and it needs more recovery time. Take a day or two off and make sure you are getting to bed before 10pm. The period between 10pm-2am is where most of the physical restoration happens.

• **Elevated Resting Heart Rate**. Take your pulse every morning before you get out of bed. This will change as you increase your fitness and should slowly decrease. If you find an unusually elevated resting heart rate, it is a sign of stress.

Take it easy for a few days and get more rest. Pushing through when your resting heart rate is elevated will almost certainly result in injury or illness.

- **Sustained Muscle Soreness.** If you do a super hard workout or extra long mileage it is normal for your muscles to be a little sore the next day-maybe even 2 days later but if soreness continues longer than this or if you start to notice you are getting muscles soreness doing not too much, it may be a sign you are just not recovering as well.

    It may be time to take a day off. Also make sure your fluid intake is good and double check your diet is full of healthy nutrients. If soreness persists, consider getting a sports massage. This helps flush out all the accumulated lactic acid, increases the circulation and muscle extensibility. Professional athletes get a sports massage after nearly every workout

- **Change in personality.** It is a common sign of over training for people to become overly irritable, stressed or depressed. It is due to inadequate recovery, hormonal changes and poor nutrition. Be aware of this and try to keep everything in balance. Remember you are doing this for fun and to enhance your life not ruin it!

Chapter 12: Putting It All Together Easily

So hopefully by now, you have already learned a lot and have a great understanding of what is involved in triathlon and how to train. If you have already done a few triathlons and know the basics, hopefully you have gained a few golden nuggets you can implement immediately. Remember even if you have heard of something before but you aren't doing it- then you don't really know it.

If there is something you know you should do –make sure you schedule it and do it.
It will separate you from everyone else.
Mostly – any changes you need to make will just be doing things a bit differently-smarter- rather than taking much more time!

There are four main reasons for failure in triathlon in my opinion

All the reasons listed below should not apply for any of you because you have read this book!

- Poor transitions

- Failure to practice at brick sessions (where you bike first then run straight away)

- Skipping workouts

- Poor nutrition

These are all poor excuses for failure and just show lack of planning and lack of doing what matters. Remember training is the art of turning your weaknesses into strengths.

Training is practicing the things in your precious spare time that will make the most difference to your event.

If you are already a great cyclist, you will probably not get a whole lot more out of going on another three-hour steady state ride. You will make up massive time by practicing a brick session and doing a one-hour cycle plus an immediate 30 - minute run.

Remember, time is precious- think about each week in advance.

Plan out what you must do, what you must achieve this week and add in what will make the biggest difference. Of course if you are training for the Ironman, you will need to devote a LOT of time to training. However if you are doing sprint or Olympic distance you can get away with training 5-10 hours a week. Just focus on training smart.

Try to keep some training kit with you in your car or office in case an opportunity arises. For example a client cancels a meeting and you have a two-hour gap in your day. You could go for a one-hour run, have a quick shower, some lunch and be back in the office, refreshed and energized.

If you have to take little Johnny to the pool, use the time to do a 30-minute swim session yourself. You will still have time to see his last few laps where he turns and waves at you and you will feel great.

If you are going to meet the girls after work at 7.30pm for a few drinks on Friday after work, tell them you will be there at 830pm. Go to the gym first. Do a 30-minute strength session and meet them afterwards. No one will mind and most will be envious of your discipline.

Just remember to make time for you and do not let another year pass where you do not achieve something for yourself, something you are really proud of!

There are different stages of training. You cannot train hard at every session but you should not do long, slow plods all the time either. The trick is to keep mixing it up and challenging your body. The trick is also learning to peak at the right time for your race.

Here is an idea of the stages of training and what to focus on at each stage.

Five main stages of training

Base Training

Many women go wrong right here at the start. They do not have the patience to do base training. This is the longer, slower training that some people see as slightly dull!

The aim is to build your aerobic capacity. This is one of the biggest factors in triathlon that will affect your racing. Without a good foundation, you will break down, burn out or get injured later in the season.

For 12 weeks or so you will work in the aerobic zone, teaching your body to burn fat instead of sugar for fuel. This is lower intensity training. So either train at a level you feel comfortable without being breathless or strap a heart rate monitor on (These are very cheap these days). After you build your base, you can focus on adding speed and power and training at anaerobic levels.

To calculate your aerobic heart rate zone:

Take 180 minus your age. If you are unfit at the moment, take 5 beats from this number.

If you already train 5-7 times a week, add 5 beats to this number.

This number is your upper limit. In this phase you are not training to the point of burning muscles or gasping for breath. You are teaching your body to burn fat. You may feel this is very easy without much perceived effort. This is correct – keep going!

For the first 12 weeks of the season, you should not go above this heart rate. Try to keep within 80% of it. So if your maximum heart rate is 150bpm, try to stay 120-150bpm for 12 weeks. Walk up the hills if you have to, put the bike in a small chain ring. Do not cheat!

Build phase

In the build phase you have built your aerobic engine. You now focus on "switching on" the fast twitch fibers in your muscles. You will now be adding speed work and increasing the intensity and volume of your training. You will still be including some lower intensity sessions each week as easy recovery workouts and to maintain your aerobic base.

Interval training will increase your speed, strength, lactic acid threshold and fast twitch fibers. Each speed session should have about 15-25 minutes of high heart rate work in it throughout the session.

So you may be doing 8 x 1000 meters running or 7 x 2 minutes on the bike; 3 x 1minutes sprints.

Doing 5-10 minutes is not enough; doing 30-35 minutes is too much.

As a general rule you should be doing 2 sessions per week of this. Train on the bike one day and run and swim the other day.

Please note that each one may take 2-3 days to recover from. Remember still apply gradual increases in intensity. This is the phase where you are at high risk of injury. Continue to listen to your body. Make sure your technique is good.

Start to ease off the weights room now and focus more on sports-specific strength.

For example use hill running and hill repeats on the bike as your resistance work, so it is specific to your sport.

When you do speed work, your body releases hormones, which build new muscle tissue

However if you do too many weeks in a row of hard, high intensity work, your muscles will start to break down. So keep checking your training diary and monitor your performances.

Start the first one at an easy pace then build the pace with each interval. If at the end you feel your form and technique slipping, ease off the speed again as you do not want to practice bad habits. Keep good form at all times.

Lactate Threshold

Some of you will have heard of "lactate threshold" and "training at your lactate threshold".

Lactic Acid Threshold (LT) is the highest intensity at which the body can recycle lactic acid as quickly as it is produced. At this intensity, you are working very hard, but can still maintain exercise because lactic acid levels in the blood and muscles are steady, not increasing. The body can still get rid of the lactic acid fast enough.

However pushing your body beyond this threshold just slightly, causes lactic acid to build up and brings premature fatigue and delayed recovery. This is that familiar feeling of burning in your muscles, rubbery legs and rapid breathing when you are really pushing hard. If you can train just below lactate threshold; you will be teaching your body to produce less lactic acid and remove it faster. This will mean you are able to produce more force without fatigue.

To work out your lactate threshold, simply monitor your heart rate as you exercise with a heart rate monitor. Notice the point at which your breathing changes and legs start to burn. Observe this on a few runs and bike rides. It will be around the same place.

The other way to do it is in running. Warm up for 10 minutes, then run a 30-minute time trial. Your average heart rate for the last 20 minutes is your lactate threshold.

If you train below this most of the time you will be able to continue for longer.

Most competitors use this in racing as well to make sure they do not "blow up" during the race and are unable to continue.

Peak Phase

In the peak phase you aim to consolidate the fitness and performance gains you have made. In this phase you reduce your workload volume but the intensity is maintained or increased. You may be looking at things like maintaining power output for a defined period.

This is where you start to understand what your race pace is. This time can be as long as 8 weeks so during these 4-8 weeks you can do some time trials at race pace to see how you handle the speed and intensity.

You will also test and clarify what fuel you will need during a race. It may be that you use a particular drink on the bike during lower intensity but when you increase the pace it may not agree with you and you may need to change.

This is the time also to simulate some race conditions and do some race distances.

Wear your race kit. Set up your bike for racing and your trainers for running with the correct race laces. Test all your kit and make sure it is comfortable.

During this phase you will feel most fatigued and tired. That is fine, you are not racing yet. Get plenty of sleep and eat well. Not every session is intense. Mix it up and make sure you are not wrecked for the next couple of days. The trick is to train hard enough so you can keep training but to make good gains based on your base phase.

The better the base you have the better your intensity will be. The saying is – the broader the base the higher the peak!

I split my training into 4 week blocks during this phase. Week 1 and 2 are less mileage often at a higher pace/ heart rate/ power, with the same number of sessions just building up some muscle endurance slowly. Week 3 is less hours and less sessions but for each discipline do a race pace session so maybe a 1k swim at race pace (or 400m if you are doing sprints), a 10 mile bike time trial and maybe a 5 or 10k run at race pace.

Do distances shorter than your race and don't go faster than you would in a race.

Week 4 is then back to longer sessions with hill repeats and more intensity. If it is a 8 week block then repeat weeks 1 to 4 but slightly faster and with more muscle endurance.

During this time you will do more brick sessions and you should be using your race bike if you have one.

In this block it would be great if you could do a shorter race to practice if possible, don't worry about times just do it, enjoy and make mistakes so you learn for your key race of the year. If it is your first race season this section is quite technical.

Don't stress about it too much, just get some volume in and do some interval training. Get used to the equipment, the distance, transitions and bricks. Keep a training diary then start to build in these phases to your training program the following year.

Racing Phase

In this phase you are participating in races. You are ready. You are using maximum effort in the race. Depending on the distance, you will taper for a certain period of time before the race. Tapering is backing off training and getting ready to race. For sprint maybe a week of much shorter sessions and low intensity is about right, for 70.3 half Ironman, do a 10 day-2week taper and for Ironman distance 2 weeks plus.

This is the time to hold back and keep calm, get good sleep, practice your transitions, plan and prepare and get your kit ready for racing.

The goal is to get to race day pumped and ready to take on the world. You should feel energized and nervous but ready to go. I often do a small brick session the day before a race so my legs don't go to sleep, 20 minutes or so on the bike then a 15-minute run, nice and easy just to keep the legs alive. If you are at a big well-organized race and you can swim in the lake, do so and get used to the water temperature and course the day before.

This phase could well last for months as you may be doing multiple races in a season. If so keep the intensity high, make sure you recover properly after a big race.

Set races out in order of importance and label them A, B and C races. Plan your race schedule around your A race and work towards it. Use B and C races as experience. Don't stress about times too much. Just enjoy them. Use the experience and get better.

If there is a big gap between races, go back and do a little base then build like before just on shorter timescales to keep your fitness up.

Recovery Phase

The other aspect of training that is rarely mentioned is recovery!

Recovery is where your body adapts to the stress placed on it from exercise, your energy systems develop and your muscles grow. Build into your program at least one day off training.

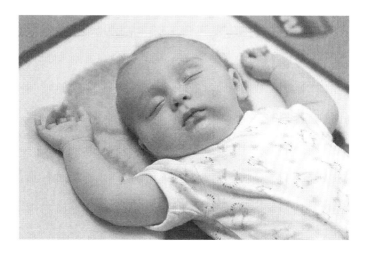

If you are starting from fresh, build in at least two days off.

As you move from your build phase into your speed work, start doing some higher intensity. Build in easier training weeks where you may do 60% the training volume of the previous weeks. This will prevent burn out and injury.

Training Zones

If you have been around training and sports for a while you will probably have come across training zones. These are heart rate zones that you work at during different stages in your training. I have provided you a sample 6-week plan as an example for you to play with.

This is not to follow to the letter. As I have already said for some of you 8 weeks will be base phase anyway. It depends how fit you are already.

This plan is a sample for someone already averagely fit who wants to do a sprint triathlon in 6 weeks. (Remember it is not the only way to train. It is just an example.)

You'll work out about 3 hours per week in the first two weeks, close to 5 hours in weeks three and four, 5 hours and 45 minutes in the fifth week, and just 1 hour and 45 minutes leading up to your race. Each intensity level, or training "zone," corresponds to a specific target heart rate in relation to your maximum heart rate (sometimes calculated as 220 minus your age).

Zone I: Training Zone I workouts should be performed at 50-60 percent of maximum heart rate. This should feel easy. Your breathing should be slightly elevated, but you should be able to hold a conversation without trouble.

Zone II: Training Zone II workouts should be performed at 60-70 percent of maximum heart rate. This is a moderately easy pace. Your breathing will feel more labored, but you should still be able to talk.

Zone III: Training Zone III workouts should be performed at 70-80 percent of maximum heart rate. This is a moderate pace. It'll be hard to hold a conversation—you can spit out a few words at a time.

Zone IV: Training Zone IV workouts should be performed at 80-90 percent of maximum heart rate. This is a moderately hard pace. You'll be struggling to talk. But remember—it's not all out. You should still be able to maintain this pace for around 20-40 minutes.

Example Training Plan

For your reference, here is an example of a beginners training plan for a sprint triathlon. It is only for reference and will not be suitable for many of you. But if you have never done anything like this before, it will give you a general idea of how to structure one.

Obviously as I pointed out before, your base training might be twelve weeks by itself- especially if you are doing a longer triathlon. So please adapt it to your existing fitness level, your goals, your planned races timings and your planned race distances.

This plan is a six-week plan for a sprint triathlon.

Week 1

> **Monday**: Rest
> **Tuesday**: Swim for 30 minutes in Zone I
> **Wednesday**: Run for 40 minutes in Zone I; strength train for 20 minutes
> **Thursday**: Rest
> **Friday**: Rest

Saturday: Bike for 60 minutes in Zone I; strength train for 20 minutes

Sunday: Swim for 15 minutes in Zone I

Week 2

Monday: Rest

Tuesday: Swim for 30 minutes in Zone II

Wednesday: Run for 40 minutes in Zone II; strength train for 20 minutes

Thursday: Rest

Friday: Rest

Saturday: Bike for 60 minutes in Zone II; strength train for 20 minutes

Sunday: Swim for 15 minutes in Zone I

Week 3

Monday: Rest

Tuesday: Swim for 30 minutes in Zone II

Wednesday: Run for 30 minutes in Zone III; strength train for 40 minutes

Thursday: Swim for 30 minutes in Zone I; bike for 60 minutes in Zone III

Friday: Rest

Saturday: Brick workout: Bike for 50 minutes in Zone I and run for 20 minutes in Zone II

Sunday: Strength train for 20 minutes

Week 4

Monday: Rest

Tuesday: Swim for 30 minutes in Zone II

Wednesday: Run for 40 minutes in Zone II; strength train for 40 minutes

Thursday: Swim for 40 minutes in Zone II; bike for 60 minutes in Zone III

Friday: Rest

Saturday: Brick workout: Bike for 50 minutes in Zone I and run for 20 minutes in Zone II

Sunday: Strength train for 20 minutes

Week 5

Monday: Rest

Tuesday: Swim for 40 minutes in Zone III

Wednesday: Bike for 30 minutes in Zone I; run for 45 minutes in Zone II; strength train for 40 minutes

Thursday: Bike for 60 minutes in Zone II

Friday: Rest

Saturday: Brick workout/test triathlon: Swim for 30 minutes in Zone I, bike for 50 minutes in Zone II, and run for 30 minutes in Zone I

Sunday: Strength train for 20 minutes

Week 6

Monday: Rest

Tuesday: Bike for 40 minutes in Zone I

Wednesday: Swim for 25 minutes in Zone I

Thursday: Run for 20 minutes in Zone I

Friday: Rest

Saturday: Swim for 15 minutes in Zone I; bike for 15 minutes in Zone I

Sunday: Race day

Taper

The taper is one of the mysteries of an athlete. In theory it sounds brilliant. Great, a whole week off training before your event, excellent!

In practice it is very hard to do as you have put in so much work, so much training and you feel like it is all going to waste. You imagine all your competitors are still out there doing some extra hill sessions.

However you cannot cheat a taper. In the week before a race you need to allow your muscles to re-fuel and feel fresh and you should be gagging to get out there at the start line.

Also when you do this you will notice you feel sluggish, lethargic and tired. This is NORMAL! Allow yourself to repair from hard training weeks guilt free.

How long to taper for varies according to the race you are preparing for. In general, for a sprint distance allow one week, for an Olympic distance allow 10 days, for a half ironman allow 2 weeks, for an Ironman allow 4 weeks.

This does not mean you stop everything for 4 weeks. It means gradually reducing volume and intensity of training.

It also means not filling every spare minute with other stuff you may have neglected during your training! Rest means rest!

Use the time to focus on your positive visualization, your flexibility and your technique.

Do easy sessions. Make sure you are hydrated and eating well.

Off Season

What should I do in the off-season?

Some people do nothing, get out of shape, put on weight and lose all the benefits they gained during the year. Getting back to race fitness is such a hard slog again, this is not recommended!

You certainly do need a break. Do all the things you love to do. Do unstructured sport. Go skiing. Play with the kids. Try rollerblading. Have fun! Try new activities. Meet up with old friends.

The off-season is a great time to work on your weaknesses. For example if your run was hampered this year with ongoing Achilles problems and calf tears, go and see a sports physiotherapist or a running coach to look at your running technique. Look at your muscle flexibility and strength and address this problem now.

Do not ignore it or wait until next season starts and go through all the agony again of dealing with ongoing injuries and missing training.

If your bike is uncomfortable, get a specialized bike fit assessment done or take some time and buy a new one.

It is important in triathlon to peak at the right times. If you go off and train really hard in the winter and impress everyone with your January times, it is likely that you will be burnt out by the summer and miss races through injury. Certainly keep your fitness up but do have some time off. Work on your flexibility and your core muscles.

The off-season is also a good time to work on your all-body strength as well.

Get to the gym and make sure you are stronger next year than this year.

Chrissie Wellington (four time World Ironman champion) speaks of the joy of "stripping down" on her blog. This does not mean naked training! But it does mean training for the pure fun of it – without analyzing heart rates, power outputs, split times and the weight of her water bottles. She said the joy of just running or cycling without all the gadgets is fantastic after a season.

In fact she recalls with fondness her first race:

"When I did my first ironman in 2007, I borrowed my team mate's tri shorts...I didn't have a swim skin – I simply wore my swimsuit over the top of my race kit, I had training wheels, I asked an age group athlete friend about nutrition and she lent me some of her drink. And before Kona six weeks later... my pedal broke and I fixed it with industrial glue, I stayed in a two bed apartment up a 20% degree slope which I biked up every day with my shopping on my back, sleeping on a single bed that was like a trampoline, sharing a room with a Spanish guy I had never met. I hadn't had a bike fit, my sunglasses were £20 from a petrol station, I got about 2 hours shut eye the night before the race because the next door neighbors were having a full volume, ear blasting depriving domestic. And I won."

Inspirational! So do not worry if you do not have all the best gear, all the sports science manuals, all the charts and graphs at your fingertips. Simply do what needs to be done – and that is train!

Start training now then come back and start your training journal straight away. Re-focus on your goals and the races you have planned this season and remember to enjoy it! Have fun and be proud of yourself!

Handy Race Day Check List

Swim

- Swim cap
- Ear plugs
- Swimming costume
- Wetsuit
- Goggles
- Spare goggles

Bike

- Water bottle
- Bike
- Helmet
- Bike shoes
- Pump

- Tire Levers
- Co2 cartridge (if necessary)
- Spare inner tubes
- Tire repair kit
- Sunglasses
- Sunscreen
- Cycling shirt, cycling shorts (or trisuit)
- Floor bike pump (before the race to get tires in perfect condition to prevent punctures and for maximum race speed)

Run

- Fuel belt
- Hat
- Running shoes
- Socks (if you choose to have them)
- Water bottle
- Towel
- Orthotics
- Sports bra

Other Essentials You Might Not Have Thought Of

Ask the organizers about whether there are lockers to leave your car keys, money, cell phone if you are going to the race solo. Of course if you have friends and family, they will come in very useful for this purpose. Other useful items you will need...

- Large plastic bags
- Small Towel
- Beach Towel
- Chamois
- Full Change of Clothes including warm gear
- Deodorant
- Baby wipes to wipe down (if there is no shower)
- Shampoo/conditioner/shower gel (if there is a shower)
- Money for post race massage, snacks or photos
- Extra hair ties
- Pair of flip flops or extra shoes
- Post Race Snacks – chocolate, snack bars, energy drink of choice, bananas, nuts
- Lipstick (for podium photos!!)
- Camera
- Race tickets
- Hotel Tickets
- Airline tickets

- Passport if necessary
- Directions to the hotel/to the race
- Chain lube
- Toilet paper
- Head light (if doing ironman!)
- Heart rate monitor
- Wrist watch

The Rules Of Racing

You do not want to do all that training, discipline and early nights and strict nutrition to get disqualified during the race!

There is a densely worded race booklet 25-30 pages long depending on the version you get, which you are free to read and digest if you want. However I suggest you spend the time training and skim through this summary I have prepared for you!

Don't litter

You will be taking on drinks, gels and protein bars during the race depending on your distance. If you are seen throwing the empty packets on the street, you will be penalized some time. If you can't reach the pocket in your shirt, simply tuck it up under your lycra shorts leg. No problem. Do not suffer unnecessary time penalties. This is just foolish.

No IPod

For safety's sake no music is allowed to be blasting in your ears. If you need music to train, make sure you do a few weeks towards the end of your training without music, prior to the race to get used to the silence.

Focus on your body, your breathing and positive affirmations as you get closer and closer to the finish line with every step and every pedal stroke. A good motto to remember is "do nothing new on race day".

No external assistance

Whilst your family and friends can be there cheering you on from the sidelines, they cannot give you any advantage. They cannot hand you a drink bottle or a sun hat or anything. The race must be completed by yourself.

Keep your own pace

Further to point 3, your family, friends or coach cannot shout your time from the sidelines or run alongside you to pace you or, I repeat, give you any help whatsoever. Make sure they understand this. You do not want to be disqualified because someone thought they would try to be "helpful".

Swim around the Buoy

This is very important. Sometimes the race can seem like a washing machine. Adrenalin is high and everyone is converging on the same spot, trying to take the quickest line. Whatever happens, do not cut the corner. You MUST swim around the buoy.

Do not cycle in the transition area

Once you grab your bike after the swim, you will be focused on getting on your bike as soon as possible. Do not be tempted to jump too early. You must pass the mount line. Jonathan Brownlee received a penalty in the Olympics for doing this and it probably cost him a silver medal.

Buckle your helmet

Officials are very strict on this one. You cannot even be fiddling with your strap as you mount your bike. My advice is to put your helmet on and buckle it properly before you even touch your bike or it could be instant disqualification.

No drafting

Drafting behind a fellow cyclist means you work 30% less. The rule is 1 meter to the left and right and 7 meters behind is the zone. Once you are in this zone you have 15 seconds to pass or you will be in trouble. If you are wondering how much 7 meters is, think 3 bike lengths. Drafting is a huge advantage and not allowed.

(Drafting in the swim is legal as discussed in the swim chapter)

At transition 2, do NOT ride to the rack

You may have guessed this anyway from rule 6 above but whilst it may be tempting to cruise to the rack, you must get off your bike at the dismount line and walk or jog your bike to the rack. You must keep your helmet on until the bike has been racked. Do not take it off when you dismount.

Stay on the course

Make sure you read the course directions before the race. Also pay attention to race signs and the marshals when on the bike and run legs. Do not cut any corners or come off the path.

Training Principles Summary

Congratulations for reading this far!

You definitely have the discipline and dedication to make it as a triathlete.

We have gone through a huge amount of information. There is a lot to absorb and take in. Here is a brief summary of the major points.

Do not get caught up in the detail. Every chapter you can return to again and again as it becomes relevant. It will mean different things to you at different stages of your training.

You have a good overview now and will already know more about triathlon than the majority of people, so remember:

- Make every session count
- Include enough rest – listen to your body
- Have an easy training week once a month
- Mix up your training sessions between short, hard, long and slow.

Training correctly will improve you as an athlete in so many ways:

- Cardiovascular system: efficient delivery of oxygen to the muscles and a stronger heart
- Your muscles increase the supply of blood vessels, bringing nutrients and taking away waste products and mitochondria (energy cells)
- Stronger joints, ligaments and bones
- Improved running, biking and swimming technique
- Improved metabolic system – your body becomes better able to convert fat, carbohydrate and protein to energy

- Improved mental strength and focus

And remember to celebrate at the end!

Be Yourself, Find Yourself and Be True to Yourself

Remember nurture yourself first and you will have more vitality and energy to give to others. You CAN do this and still have enough time for your family, work and social life.

Triathlon has overtaken marathon as the new challenge to do! You will get amazing bragging rights, develop a lean, toned body, find a whole new gang of friends, gain incredible self confidence and thoroughly enjoy the whole process.

Stand up and be a powerful example to your children, your partner and your work colleagues. Grow into a stronger woman, a goal achiever, one who overcomes obstacles and does what others merely talk about. Live with purpose and with action.

Practice your training on a daily basis. It is what you do each and every day that counts. Not just the show time at a race! It is the getting up 40 minutes early to cycle before work. It is the going for a jog even though it is raining. It is the stretching for 15 minutes when you get in from a run. It is the discipline to say "no" to your 10-mile run written in your program because you feel a "tweak" in your calf.

It is the sum of all these things that will determine who you are as an athlete.

Are you full of excuses "why not?" and "I pulled out of the race because..."

Or

Are you full of results and achievements, bursting with pride when you ring up your mum or dad to share it with them or when you see your kids and partner at the finish line cheering you in?

It is building a team of support all around you all pulling in the same direction to help you become a better, person, a better athlete, an all-round winner.

So jump right in and enjoy the tremendous journey that awaits you.

. . . . .

I am so excited for you and can't wait to hear your stories and results.

Please contact me at charlotte1@triathlon-hacks.com

Let me know of your results and if you have any questions along the way, I am always delighted to help

If you enjoyed the book, would you please spare a minute and write me an honest review.

It makes a big difference and I would really appreciate it.

I wish you well in your training and your triathlon adventure.

Stay updated and continue to receive the latest information and incredible training tips

http://www.triathlon-hacks.com

Click here to get your free download on **how I took 17% off my triathlon race performance by training less!**

■■■

About Charlotte:

Charlotte Campbell is an accomplished triathlete. She has successfully competed in triathlon since 2001. Charlotte is passionate about helping as many people as possible (in particular, women) to succeed in triathlon.

Charlotte is a writer, author, blogger and coach. She has helped over 1237 clients so far achieve far more than they thought possible, overcome their training plateaus and overcome their fears.

She does not believe in living within a comfort zone and believes everyone (including her!) can benefit from a gentle nudge in the right direction.

Charlotte has degrees in science and physical therapy. She writes for various newspaper and health magazines and has been interviewed on the radio.

She is most passionate about simplifying triathlon training into a program almost everyone can do within the constraints of a normal life. She believes in training smarter, not longer.

Charlotte loves to go shopping, travel and spend time with her family. She loves being fit and active and spending time outdoors.

Swim Blow out til head above
water
Lock core shoulder to hip
Roll like a barrel
Recovery arm relaxed.
Start slow find rythym S stke
Breast stke

T1 wetsuit, date drink uries headtw
Helmet, T Shirt, socks ~~braces~~
shoes

Bike 4 laps start slow – rythm

T2 Helm off trainers, headband
Run 3 laps 1x slow
1x med
1x faster.

- powers are good
- Can swim 1k so def do 750m
- Can bike 1hr easily good cycler
good glutes
- Can run 5k easily
– There no doubt I can do this
I can do this